POSITIVE DRINKING

POSITIVE DRINKING

Control the Alcohol Before It Controls You!

KEVIN LAYE

HAY HOUSE

Australia • Canada • Hong Kong • India
South Africa • United Kingdom • United States

First published and distributed in the United Kingdom by:
Hay House UK Ltd, 292B Kensal Rd, London W10 5BE. Tel.: (44) 20 8962 1230;
Fax: (44) 20 8962 1239. www.hayhouse.co.uk

Published and distributed in the United States of America by:
Hay House, Inc., PO Box 5100, Carlsbad, CA 92018-5100. Tel.: (1) 760 431 7695 or
(800) 654 5126; Fax: (1) 760 431 6948 or (800) 650 5115. www.hayhouse.com

Published and distributed in Australia by:
Hay House Australia Ltd, 18/36 Ralph St, Alexandria NSW 2015. Tel.: (61) 2 9669 4299;
Fax: (61) 2 9669 4144. www.hayhouse.com.au

Published and distributed in the Republic of South Africa by:
Hay House SA (Pty), Ltd, PO Box 990, Witkoppen 2068. Tel./Fax: (27) 11 467 8904.
www.hayhouse.co.za

Published and distributed in India by:
Hay House Publishers India, Muskaan Complex, Plot No.3, B-2, Vasant Kunj, New Delhi
– 110 070. Tel.: (91) 11 4176 1620; Fax: (91) 11 4176 1630. www.hayhouse.co.in

Distributed in Canada by:
Raincoast, 9050 Shaughnessy St, Vancouver, BC V6P 6E5. Tel.: (1) 604 323 7100;
Fax: (1) 604 323 2600

© Kevin Laye, 2010

A catalogue record for this book is available from the British Library.

ISBN 978-1-84850-240-6

Printed and bound in the UK by CPI Bookmarque, Croydon, CR0 4TD.

All of the papers used in this product are recyclable, and made from wood grown in
managed, sustainable forests and manufactured at mills certified to ISO 14001 and/or
EMAS.

To Nicola and Samantha for making me smile and for being there to push my wheelchair when I am much older ☺

Love you both very much x

(Oh, and Jack and Bud, too)

Shakespeare goes into a pub and orders a pint and the barman tells him 'no!' and to 'get out'. Shakespeare asks 'Why?' and the barman replies, 'Because you're Bard.'

Contents

CONTENTS

Acknowledgements

In writing this, my second book, I would like to begin by first saying that this is my interpretation of the skills and techniques taught to me over the years by many great people, and I would not have put pen to paper (well, fingertips to keyboard, to be more precise) if it weren't for their generosity in sharing their knowledge and wisdom with me over time.

I would like to thank the following: Roger Callahan (creator of TFT), Gary Craig (creator of EFT), Richard Bandler and John Grinder (creators of NLP), Michael Neill (Super-coach extraordinaire), Milton Erickson (sadly deceased and possibly the greatest hypnotic mind ever). You are amazing teachers dead or alive – or maybe somewhere in-between! ☺

Hay House for their belief in my work and continued support of me; it is an honour to be part of the 'family'.

Speaking of families, my thanks to Karen, Margaret and 'da gurlz': Nicola and Samantha. Love you all. And thanks to Maria for being a big part of my life for so long.

Steve and Janet, my co-founders of the MCP Meta Changework Practitioner group and to all our trainees who have grown and blossomed into outstanding therapists of SAS therapy: 'Who cares wins.'

My thanks to all my clients, who have trusted in me to help them over the years. I learn so much from your stories, and hope I reciprocate your trust and faith in me by helping you. You also help me learn.

The Big Blue Hotel in Blackpool must also get a mention for taking such good care of me in the final days of writing this book. Oh, and for the suite. Ta lots!!

My final thanks must go, I think, to my dear friend and mentor Paul McKenna. My friend has been a constant source of inspiration to me and has always been there to support me over the years I have known him. I really have to thank him also for leaving one segment of the self-help market untouched by not bringing out a book called 'I can make you sober.' ☺ Thanks, Big P.

I guess my final, final thanks go to everyone who decided to take back control by buying and reading this book and using it. Good call, and thank you so much for trusting me. *Namaste.*

Who Is this Book for?

This is a book about taking control of alcohol *before* it can take control of you, and therefore is not a book for anyone currently diagnosed an as alcoholic. Now, having said that *(and in a way contradicting myself)*, I should point out that some of the techniques contained within this book may assist someone undergoing a programme to wean themselves off alcohol, and I have used many of the techniques in this book to treat clients who came to me with alcohol addiction issues, and indeed to treat diagnosed alcoholics.

This book contains techniques that will enable the reader to have more control over alcohol and, in many cases, other addictive substances such as legal drugs like chocolate and cigarettes, and also some illegal and more pernicious drugs. The techniques are simple to apply and rapid in their outcome, breaking the old behaviour and enabling you to install newer, better, more productive behaviours. You see, to me it seems a little odd, if not perverse, that we feel out of control, mostly due to stress, so we then fill ourselves with a drug *(in this instance alcohol)* and usually end up making ourselves totally out of control.

The book is not meant to counsel you or to be empathetic or, even worse, to analyse *(anal-lies)*, but instead offers some very direct, simple and proven techniques that will allow you to have total control in many situations, not just those where alcohol is your 'quick fix' or your chemical 'comfort zone'.

For the techniques in this book to work for you, you have to use them. It is akin to someone joining a gym and after a year complaining that they have not got any fitter, when the fact is they have not once actually been to the gym. For these techniques to have an effect, you simply need to use them.

I have made all the techniques very simple to apply, and using the minimum of time, as I also know most things don't happen because we do not have the time to do them – odd, though, how we can always make time to do things that may case us damage, like over-eat, get drunk, etc, … Hold that thought!

I have not written this book from a high moral standpoint, either. I drink, and I am in total control of how much I drink and when I drink (unless I get drunk). I am able to go weeks or sometimes months without drinking, but can also go out with a group of people whom I trust implicitly, and get totally 'off my face', and I sometimes do.

This happens, not often but occasionally, and sometimes it's fun and sometimes I pay the price for a day (or occasionally 'daze') after. If the latter happens, it comes out of a conscious choice and I am fully aware of the consequences.

The bottom line is, alcohol itself isn't bad, but its inappropriate use and the inappropriate behaviour it can manifest are bad. The simple logic is, if you are not in control of yourself, then who or what is?

I simply want to offer you choices and options, which you will either use or not use. You are as free to choose here as much as you are free to choose to be in control from now on.

In taking more control, what have you got to lose?

So, if you want to have more control now ... read on.

Are You Addicted?

OK, here is a little experiment I would invite you to do.

Get comfortable and then look at a fixed object or a spot on the wall. Avoid looking at anything bright, which may hurt your eyes, and definitely do not look at the sun (*I mean the big yellow stellar object, not any newspaper of the same name!*).

OK, while staring at the object, follow this simple instruction:

Keep your eyes open for as long as you can without blinking.

Well done. So how well did you do? Some last a few

seconds whereas a few can make it past a minute. So what is the point of this experiment? Well, you will all have reached a point where the 'only' thing you could do was to blink. You had to, there was no way you could not, unless you used matches as scaffolding to keep your eyes open, and that would have been uncomfortable and potentially dangerous.

You see, to me, an addict is someone who cannot not do a behaviour, whether it is drinking, smoking, eating (or not, in the case of anorexia).

If you have to drink and there is no other option, then you are addicted and in my opinion no longer in control. You see, you genuinely *must* blink, it's a biological need, but no one 'must' drink. Not that you can't drink, but you don't *have* to. 'Having to' is the issue here.

The technical term for this is 'bad', and you need a method to help you take that control back *now*, if not even sooner.

If that sounds good to you, then welcome to Positive Drinking and read on ...

TOTAL CONTROL
ON TAP

Total Control 'on Tap'

'A mind is like a parachute – it works best when it is open.' – Anonymous

'Beer?' asked Bob. 'Yeah, great … please,' replied Carl. 'Usual poison,' Carl continued as he went to find some seats with a good view of the TV.

Sitting down, he watched the screen without paying much notice as Bob sat adjacent to him at the table placing the beers down on the beer mats. Carl picked up his beer and took a good long drink before saying, 'Cheers, mate, I needed that.' Bob nodded as he took a mouthful and drank it down before replying, 'Mmm … first taste is always the best.' He then continued, 'Thought it might be busier in here with the game showing.' Carl shrugged a response before adding, 'Probably all at home on the couch with a curry and some cheap supermarket beer.' Bob laughed in agreement. 'Not quite the same though, is it?' he asked rhetorically. Carl downed his drink before asking, 'Another?' 'I'm OK for the minute,' responded Bob. Carl stood and headed towards the bar, saying as he went, 'Well, I need another.' Carl sat down after his trip to the bar with his next beer and took another large gulp before wiping his mouth with the back of his hand. They both looked at the screen for a while watching the pre-game pundits extol their combined wisdom and offer predictions of the outcome. As Carl finished his second pint he noticed Bob was still only halfway through his first. 'Refill?' asked Carl as he stood to go to the bar again. 'Nah, thanks, I'm fine for now,' responded Bob with a confirming shake of his head. Carl returned and sat down, drinking a third of the pint down before placing his glass on the mat.

Both got more engrossed in the game, taking occasional drinks and emptying their glasses simultaneously. 'So what do you think the score will be?' Bob asked. 'Three–One on the beer front,' laughed Carl, 'you ready for another?' 'Yeah, sure, same again please, mate' replied Bob. Carl stood up and took the empties to the bar as he headed there for the fourth time that evening. Carl returned with the refills and they both sat watching the game. An observer would have noticed Carl drinking at a much greater rate than Bob and also shouting at the telly more. Carl finished his fourth pint as half-time was called and he noticed Bob still had about a quarter of his glass still left.

Bob saw Carl's empty glass, and asked, 'Another?' 'Rude not to,' smiled Carl, so Bob got up and took his partially empty glass and Carl's empty to the bar. Bob returned with a pint for Carl and what seemed to be the same glass he'd gone up to the bar with, with a half-pint top-up. In the background the pundits were replaying the first half game 'as it should have gone according to them' and postulating about how the second half would go. 'You feeling all right, bud?' asked Carl. 'Yeah, I'm good,' Bob responded, 'Why do you ask?'

'Well, you seem to be drinking a little more slowly so I wondered if you had a bad stomach or something.'

'Nah,' Bob laughed, 'I'm on a three-pint limit tonight.'

'Really?' said Carl, looking surprised, 'Says who?'

'Says me,' said Bob. 'I've been overdoing it for a while now and I need to slow down, and a mate of mine at work showed me this technique he uses, which allows him to drink but only to a limit he sets for himself. I was really cynical at first but I've tried it a couple of times now and it really works … it's weird, but it works.' 'How's that, then?' asked Carl. 'OK, if you really want to know I'll try to explain, but you're going to really think I'm a nut job,' said Bob. 'Already do,' interjected Carl with a grin. Bob returned a grin of his own and continued, saying,

'Well, Tom at work used to come in quite often looking worse for wear … burning the candle at both ends, if you know what I mean, and a couple of times the boss "had a word" with him. This past month, though, he really seems to have got himself sorted. He's no longer late; he seems to be enjoying work a bit more and just in general looks better. I was in the coffee room with him one morning a week ago, pulling a double espresso out of the machine to make myself more alert, and Tom asked me if I had had a heavy night. "Oh, yes … again," I replied.

He smiled and said, "Yup, been there – but I'm not going there again." "How are you going to manage that?" I asked him, and he just smiled and said, "Because now I have control back, and it feels great." He then said, "I was shown this weird but effective technique recently, which allows me to set a limit in my head and stick to it, and bizarrely if I try to go past what I've set I just can't … it's like something … stops me."

"Can you show me?" I asked him. Tom replied that he would but I had to have an open mind because it looked "and felt" strange. "No stranger than I feel now," I quipped.

"OK," said Tom. "Meet me in here this afternoon at break time and I'll take you through the technique. I can't do it now as you don't look to be in any fit state. You need to recover a little."

"Probably for the best," I agreed. "3:30 OK?"

"3:30 it is, then," said Tom, "just bring an open mind with you."

With that I went back to my work waiting for the caffeine to "de-fog" my brain.

3:30

As arranged at 3:30 I went down to the cafeteria and there was Tom waiting for me as promised, and although I felt somewhat better I was intrigued by what Tom had said earlier. I had spent a large part of the day reviewing my past behaviour and why I let myself get wasted so often and so easily. I had to change my "habits". I was 32 but feeling 55 (or what I thought 55 might feel like!).

Tom leaned over and pulled out a chair for me to sit down. I sat.

"OK, let's get to it," Tom said. "Feeling better?" "Lots," I replied, "I felt rubbish this morning." "Have to be honest, you looked it," smiled Tom. "So were you celebrating anything special to get so hammered?" "Just Tuesday," I laughed in response. "No, seriously, nothing ... I seem to have just got into the habit of overdoing it a bit too often ... not good, huh?" I asked. Silence. "So, anyway, Tom, why are you looking so fighting fit these days? You used to look how I felt earlier."

"I know," said Tom, "and one day I just realized I was sick and tired of feeling sick and tired, so I went to see this guy, a kind of therapist I guess, who taught me these weird but effective techniques." "OK, I am suitably on the edge of my seat and prepared for weird. What is this technique?"

"Well, it's called Meridian Therapy – more commonly referred to as 'tapping' therapy," said Tom. "You simply tap on some acupuncture points on the body and it enables you to feel calm and relaxed and to take control over emotions and over things that you normally use to control your emotions, like food or drink." I guess I smiled with that kind of "yeah, right" smile, because Tom continued, "and the cool thing is you can think it's a crock and it still works. It requires no belief in it or buying into it. I was a real cynic but it works for me."

"OK then," I responded. "In for a penny, in for a pound, I guess. How does it work?"

"It works very well," Tom joked with a smile, then went on, "OK, do this: think about having a drink and set a limit in your head as to how much is OK for you. When you have that figure in mind, give me a nod."

I thought for a few seconds and answered, "A few beers."

"Sorry, you need to be more specific," said Tom, "how many specifically?"

"Two then," I responded, "yeah, two seems right." "Fine," said Tom, "two it is. Now then, imagine being in your local pub or wherever you choose to drink, and imagine having your two beers and being fine with them and really noticing how they taste … you can do that, can't you?" "Indeed I can," I said, "years of practice."

"Now do this, then," instructed Tom. "Tap the side of your hand about 20 times. Then tap under the end of your collarbone, on the bony bit under the neck, about 10 times. Then tap under your eye (either eye) about 10 times. Then tap again on that collarbone point." I followed Tom's instructions and watched as he looked at me. "OK," he said, "now imagine trying to drink a third pint."

As I did so Tom smiled as he saw the obvious look of both distaste and pseudo-horror on my face. "Damn, that's weird," I erupted, "my throat feels like it's closing up and I can't even imagine having that drink, it's almost like I can't even picture it." "I know," said Tom, "try to override it and force yourself to drink."

"I can't, Tom, I really can't … Is that it, is that all I have to do?"

"Pretty much," said Tom, "it also seems the more you do it the more effective it gets … here, let me write down what you need to do."'

'So, Carl, that's kind of it,' Bob explained. 'Before I come out, like tonight, I just set a limit in my head of how much I want to drink and tap away, and I am not able to drink past that point. I really do have control back, and it's so easy.'

Carl had that 'yeah, right' look on his face before asking, 'So what if you *do* want to get wasted?'

'Then I can,' Bob replied, 'but, I have to be honest, that's kind of saved for special occasions now. What I like is knowing I can remember the night before and not having my work or my health or my wallet suffer like they used to. Also I can still enjoy a drink as much as anyone, but now it's on *my* terms and under my control and influence as opposed to being "under the influence".'

'Try it on me, then,' challenged Carl. 'Hmmm,' responded Bob, 'is that you or the drink talking? And,' Bob continued, 'what if it works as well on you as it does me, what will you do then?'

'Actually, no, I am serious,' Carl said, softening his tone. 'I keep getting nagged that I am drinking too much, and times are a little tighter than I'd like, so if I could save a little then that would be a good thing for me.'

'Game's starting again,' Bob said. 'Imagine that pint being your last tonight, look at it and drink a little of it to see how it is.'

Carl took a swig. 'Tastes good to me,' he responded. 'OK, then,' Bob said, 'knowing you want to stop after this pint, tap where I tell you to.'

After Carl and Bob finished doing the exercise they returned to watching the game. 'Glad it's quiet in here tonight; if people were watching that they would have thought we were a couple of loons doing that tapping stuff,' laughed Carl.

As the game came to a close with a 2–0 result, Carl took the last mouthful of his drink and Bob did likewise. 'Another?' asked Bob. A mix of confusion and mild disgust came over Carl's face as he answered, 'No thanks, mate.'

'What happens if you think about drinking another?' asked Bob.

'Feels odd,' reported Carl. 'It's like I know I should be able to but I really don't want to, like there is no point, I feel I have had enough.'

'That's you back in control then,' said Bob. 'All you need to do is use the technique. I'll email the full thing to you when I get home. Speaking of which, it's time to hit the road.'

'Thanks, bud,' said Carl. 'What a surreal evening it has been! I'll let you know how I get on.'

'Just follow the email, ' smiled Bob. 'The technique can't fail, only you can fail to do the technique. So "just do it."' 'Yes, sir,' Carl saluted. Both guys laughed and went on their separate ways home. Bob was tapping the side of his hand as he did so. So was Carl.

JEKYLL AND HYDE

Jekyll and Hyde

The Strange Case of Dr Jekyll and Mr Hyde is an interesting metaphor for many current-day addictive behaviours. Written in 1886 by Robert Louis Stevenson, it tells the story of Dr Henry Jekyll, a respected physician who unlocks a hidden, darker side he keeps secret to himself. Jekyll experiments and creates a potion that enables him to metamorphose into Edward Hyde, an evil creature devoid of any conscience. Initially Jekyll is attracted to the feelings of moral freedom that Hyde enjoys. After a period of time, however, Jekyll begins to change into Hyde involuntarily in his sleep, so he takes steps to stop becoming Hyde. These efforts are successful for some time, but then one night the urge to change overwhelms him, and while out on a nightly rampage as Hyde, he murders someone. Jekyll pledges to himself he will try harder to stop changing, however one day he changes involuntarily whilst in the park. This is the first time it happens in the daytime. Jekyll is aware his potion to reverse the transformation is beginning to run out, and is fully aware that he will soon become Hyde permanently. He writes a final letter as Jekyll, knowing that by the time his friends read it, Henry Jekyll will be no more and Edward Hyde will have taken over forever.

As I said, this seems a relevant metaphor for many of today's binge-drink issues. Stevenson's story is one of a 'split personality' enhanced and embellished with the drinking of a potion. Once drunk, Jekyll loses all inhibitions and any sense of moral being. He enjoys this aspect of his personality, even though when confronted with the grim reality of it when he is not in his drink-induced altered state, he is appalled by the way he has behaved and the reports of the trails of devastation he has left behind him. This does not stop him repeating the behaviour, though, even when he swears he will. The urge once again gets too much and the consequence is the height of violent criminal behaviour. Ah! But it wasn't Jekyll, it was Hyde, or rather the drink that turns him into Hyde. The drink is the excuse, the reason, something to blame. It is the drink that makes him lose control. He would never do those things as the sober, respectable Dr Henry Jekyll.

Sound familiar?

Today, our modern surveillance society enables us to see the behaviour of the Mr Hyde 'hidden' in each of us, which we can 'hide' away until the demon drink makes us demonic. CCTV footage is shown on the news, and even on those special programmes dedicated to displaying the worst of human behaviour, where police roam around with 'live' cameras to record the part of us we like to 'Hyde' away until we drink, when 'it' is free to do what it wishes with the moral freedom enjoyed by Edward Hyde. We have all seen the pictures in the papers of the drunken ladette, walking around the streets with her knickers around her ankles, or the innocent man walking alone and being set upon by thugs, or even the less violent aspect with people evacuating their bodies of bodily fluids. Ah! But the drink is to blame. The drink is in control, isn't it?

Now I am sure some of you are thinking I am giving drinkers a hard time here, and showing only the extremes of the worst behaviour – and yes, I agree, I am. Jekyll and Hyde is, however, just a story, a metaphor. I do hope, though, as you read it, that the other you, the 'hidden' you, as in your unconscious mind, will take on board the story's true meaning. Jekyll had control until he lost control. We all have a potential Hyde within us to some degree.

Who would you like to be in control?

Note

There is an exercise, a self-test that anyone can do, which is explained for you in the 'Back in Control!' chapter later in this book (see page 122). It enables you to determine, through a simple self-testing procedure, if something (in this case drink, though it can be used to test anything) is OK for you or not. You can either read the rest of the book until you come to it, or take a look now and try it out for yourself. Use it and I promise it will make a difference to your choices and your levels of control. Enjoy the Yes/No technique. ☺

HAVING A 'SKIN-FULL'

Having a 'Skin-full'

Louise walked into the beauty salon, removing her sunglasses as she crossed the threshold. She squinted her eyes before putting them back on and heaving a sigh of relief. 'Hi,' said the receptionist, far too perkily for Louise's liking, 'have a seat and Jan will be with you in a minute or two.' Louise duly took a seat and shrugged off her coat, then proceeded to remove her sunglasses again, this time with a bit more caution. Once removed she placed them in the case she had taken from her bag before putting it back again.

She flicked through the stack of magazines on the table before selecting one and beginning to read it through squinted eyes, as her vision was very blurry. After half a paragraph she gave up and put the magazine back. After a few minutes Jan, her stylist and friend, emerged from behind a screen, pulling it back to reveal a woman in her late thirties, Louise guessed, and who looked pretty damn good, Louise decided. Jan caught Louise's eye and held up a couple of fingers to indicate how long she would be. Louise nodded in acknowledgement, mouthing 'OK' at the same time. Jan led the woman to the desk and got her coat, and as she helped her on with it they exchanged a few words and a giggle before she left. Jan then turned to Louise and smiled a beaming smile as she said, 'Hi, how are you?' Louise shook her head gently as she let out an 'ooph!' sound before following this up with, 'I need a new me.'

'Oh?' responded Jan. 'Come through and let's have us a little chat.' They both moved to the booths and as Louise sat down Jan pulled the screen behind them to give them some privacy. 'Go on, then,' Jan continued, 'tell me what's wrong.' 'No, I'll just sound whiney and pathetic and a moaning Minnie,' Louise replied. 'Oh, and you think I haven't heard just about everything before in these booths?' argued Jan, 'and I can't help if I don't know now, can I?'

'Well, I feel a mess,' began Louise, 'my head hurts, I feel bloaty, my skin's dry, and so is my hair, and I noticed in the pool at the weekend my first couple of cellulite bumps. I mean, c'mon, I'm not even 30 yet. It's not fair. I guess I just have very unlucky genes. Why can't I have the genes of that last woman you saw? She looked amazing, and I bet she was a good ten years older than me.'

'Oh,' said Jan, biting her lip as she did so, 'she actually just turned 50 ... sorry,' she continued as she saw Louise's face drop even more.

'So what's her secret?' asked Louise, sounding a little petulant.

'Well, I'd like to think part of it's down to me,' laughed Jan, 'I've been seeing her now for about ten years, and I can assure you it isn't her gene pool. I've seen her younger sister,' said Jan, screwing up her nose slightly, 'chalk and cheese. Oh dear, did that sound catty?'

Louise shook her head and gave a reassuring 'No' followed by a wry smile and, 'Well, maybe a little.' They both laughed.

'Well, to quote Meg Ryan in *When Harry Met Sally*, I'll have whatever she's having,' Louise caught herself, and followed by saying, 'or is that going to be way too expensive, and am I beyond repair?'

Jan laughed as she responded, 'No ... actually a lot of what makes her look so good is free.' 'Free?!' gasped Louise, 'How so?'

'Well,' responded Jan, 'the reason your skin is so dry and your hair isn't bouncy and you feel the way you do is because you are very dehydrated and, judging by your headache, and what you have said, it's probably because you have been overdoing it on the "pop" ... am I right?'

'I'm not sure,' replied Louise with a questioning look crossing her face. 'Is a couple of glasses of wine a night, to unwind, overdoing it?'

'That's not really for me to say, Louise, but you do need to listen to what your body is telling you, and it seems to be saying it needs renewing – as you put it, to give you "a new you".' Jan continued, 'Although I deal with mostly the cosmetic and external side of things, it seems obvious a lot of your concerns are coming from an internal source. Our bodies are like computers and there is a saying in geek land: "Garbage in, garbage out." If you put rubbish in, it comes out somewhere – and it's obvious it's not healthy.'

'Makes sense, I guess,' admitted Louise. 'So tell me what this magic tonic is, then, that's FREE!?'

'Water,' said Jan, in a matter-of-fact manner. 'It really is a magic elixir or life and it's on tap, excuse the pun, 24/7. It does amazing things to keep us healthy.'

'Such as?' questioned Louise.

'Well, let me explain why alcohol may be unhealthy first,' replied Jan. 'Every glass of wine contains around 125 to 150 calories. That's equivalent to a couple of bars of chocolate a day if you think about it.' Louise, by the look on her face, obviously was.

Jan continued, 'Your body's largest organ is your skin, and alcohol not only dehydrates you but it also deprives your skin of certain vital vitamins and other nutrients. And what's worse, if you carry this on over time you can develop other more serious issues, for example rosacea, which begins with mild flushing and blushing but can soon lead to broken blood vessels and sometimes permanent scarring. You see, alcohol dilates the small blood vessels under the skin, hence a drinker's ruddy cheeks. If this goes unchecked, it can lead to thin red veins, which in turn can clump into small red studded bumps and pus spots.' Jan saw the horror creeping over Louise's face but carried on relentlessly, 'It's also what makes you bloated and makes your face look puffy, and many believe that the toxins in alcohol contribute to the build-up of cellulite. Then there are the other side-effects: people who drink too much and get hungover don't smell too good. Your liver metabolizes about 90 to 95 per cent of the alcohol you drink, while the remainder exits your body via your breath, your sweat and your urine.'

'No shit!' said Louise looking mortified.

'Ah, good point,' Jan carried on. 'Alcohol can be a contributing factor to bloating of the stomach and possibly IBS – and *constipation*,' Jan's face broke into an 'eek' smile followed immediately by Louise saying, 'I'm doomed.'

'Not at all,' assured Jan, 'cutting down a little on the "pop" and drinking plenty of good old H_2O will soon have you sorted out.'

'You think so?' asked Louise.

'I know so,' confirmed Jan with a firm nod. 'Water will help flush acquired toxins from your system and rebalance your natural hydration. It also aids the liver and kidneys, to metabolize the alcohol you have in your system, and makes you feel full so you are less likely to get alcohol-induced munchies after a few drinks, and by default you will probably drink much less wine as your system feels hydrated and, well, just "better". You see, there is no downside to drinking water. Oh! And it has zero calories.'

'That really appeals,' smiled Louise, 'and with the zero cost, what's to lose?'

'Precisely…,' said Jan, 'right, now, let's get your massage started.'

'Massage!' cried Louise. 'After that information overload, I think I need a drink!'

'Sure, what can I get for you?' enquired Jan.

'Oh, water please,' laughed Louise. 'Make it a double!'

'Think I'll join you,' said Jan with a smile, as she drew back the screen to go and get the drinks.

WHAT A STATE TO GET INTO

What a State to Get Into

One of the beliefs of NLP (Neuro-Linguistic Programming) is that all of our behaviour is the result of the state we are in, and that our state is governed mostly by our physiology and our internal dialogue (*as in the things we say to ourselves*).

To demonstrate this, try this exercise.

> Sit or stand and drop your shoulders and look at the floor. Slouch a little and breathe shallow breaths. Now just say 'No' over and over again in your head about 20 times. Then stop and assess how you feel … pretty negative, I bet.

OK, we don't want to have you in that state, so do this:

> Stand or sit upright with your shoulders back, almost
> military style, look slightly upwards and breathe
> deeply and fully. Now say 'Yes' in an excited tone in
> your head about 20 times. Now stop and assess how
> you feel … pretty good and positive, I guess.

So what if you were able to access that last state easily and feel good 'for no reason'. I mean, think about it. How often have you felt bad or negative and when asked why you say, 'Oh, no reason.' So if you are able to feel bad for no reason, why not learn to feel good for no reason? What's to lose?

We are able to achieve this by using a very powerful NLP technique known as *anchoring*. We already have many anchors in our life, both positive and negative. A song on the radio can bring back memories of good times in the past or even heartbreak if it is attached to someone you loved but who has now left you. These are *auditory anchors*. I can still remember from the tone of my grandmother's voice when she called my name whether it was time for tea or if I was in big trouble. I'm sure you have had the same kinds of experiences.

We can picture in our mind someone who bothers us, and as soon as we picture them it can make us angry; likewise we can picture someone and get all gooey at the thought of them. These are *visual anchors*.

Anchors are everywhere in life, and they, as much as anything, control our states and thus our behaviours. Any routine behaviour that creates a response is an anchor, such as time at the gym, soaking in the bath, walking the dog, or even a drink or two in your local bar. Anchors can develop into habitual behaviour, which if positive for us is good, and if negative for us is obviously bad, even though the intention of the behaviour may seem to be positive.

So can we anchor positive states easily? … Well, yes, we can.

Think of a time when you've felt totally relaxed and calm. Close your eyes and see what you saw, hear what you heard, and feel how good you felt. Then make the images bigger and brighter and the sounds louder and bolder, and flood the feelings through your body. Notice the changes happening inside and, when you begin to feel really calm, squeeze the tips of your index finger and thumb on your right hand together. Then open your eyes and think of tea and toast or something to break the calm state.

Now squeeze your fingertip and thumb together again and notice what happens. You should easily get back the calm feeling you had a moment ago.

If you keep on doing this, it forms a habit – and that means you can begin to feel relaxed and calm whenever you like, because you will have anchored a 'resource state' that you can access any time by squeezing your finger and thumb together. How easy is that?

If you didn't quite get it first time, then try again but this time amplify the images, sounds and feelings and then, as they reach a peak, squeeze. The timing of 'fixing' this anchor is important.

Think of a time you've felt supremely confident. Close your eyes, see what you saw, hear what you heard, and feel how good you felt. Then make the images bigger and brighter and the sounds louder and bolder, and flood the feelings through your body. Notice the changes happening inside and, when you begin to feel really calm, squeeze your fingertip and thumb on your right hand together. Add the confidence to the calm you had before and let them mix, and squeeze again. Then open your eyes and think of something different as you break your finger and thumb apart and, after a moment, squeeze finger and thumb together again and feel what happens.

Did you get both feelings (calm and confidence)? If so, then that's great. This is called *stacking anchors*. If you didn't quite get it, then try again.

The best way to get good at something is to practise, and the best way to practise is to practise. An interviewer once asked golfing legend Gary Player if his game wasn't largely down to luck. Player responded, 'Well, I find the more I practise, the luckier I get.'

Practice is the key. You see, you may have developed a habit of drinking to relieve stress or to make you feel good, but when it becomes a habit or a dependency, then it can also become a problem, too.

Wouldn't it be good to have some other resources you could access and use instead to feel good?

Oh, and please don't be concerned that I am trying to turn you into some 'Pollyanna' type who can only see the positive in everything. Not at all. You have my permission to have a crappy day; however I invite you to ask yourself who has given you the rubbish day. Who, when you woke up, stood over your bed and said, 'Good morning, here is the day of crap I am presenting you with, here is your box of crap for the day ... enjoy'? Who was it who did that to you? So, have the day of your choosing. Remember, though, your state governs your behaviour, and your behaviour affects everyone you come into contact with.

Now, here is another use for anchors. If you find you are addicted to something such as alcohol and you don't wish to be, you can use a little trick called *collapsing anchors*. To do this you need to think of the thing you want to get rid of or have less compulsion around, and also think of something that repulses or disgusts you. Ideally this will be something you have experienced. It can be a food or smell, or anything as long as it repulses you.

> Think of the thing you like but want to like less and squeeze together the thumb and little finger of your right hand (we don't want to stack this on the previous good anchors). Amplify it till it feels nice and you create some desire.

OK, now think of the thing that repulses you, and imagine the smell or taste and being forced to eat or drink it, and do this until you feel borderline nausea as you imagine ingesting it. Now on your left hand, squeeze the little finger and thumb together until the feeling of disgust reaches a peak. Then switch back to the right-hand little finger and thumb anchor of the thing you like for a second or two and, just as you begin to get a pleasure signal, switch back to the left-hand nausea anchor of thumb and little finger. Once again when you feel total disgust and feel nauseous, switch back for a second to the right-hand anchor. Keep switching back and forth in this manner about ten times, then squeeze both little finger and thumb anchors on both hands at the same time, and see what happens. The repulsion should make the desire collapse, so you're no longer hankering after the thing you have chosen to have more control over.

From now on it will be very easy to 'fire off' your anchor of disgust on your left hand every time you think of the thing of which you once desired too much.

It is always important to end by firing off good anchors to allow you to feel good 'for no reason at all'. After all, we wouldn't want to encourage you to have a rubbish day for no reason now, would we?

So how would your life be if you learned to control your state and in turn your behaviour? How good would you feel? How many good feelings could you cope with? How much money might you save, and what could you do with that? How good would it feel to have total control? Can you see the value in having that control … or not?

If you can, good … anchor that feeling and feel good for no reason. ☺

END-OF-THE-PIER
PRESSURE

End-of-the-Pier Pressure

The seafront at Blackpool was very, very windy, so the guys really felt the sudden calm in the air as they entered the pub. They were up on a boys-only weekend with bridegroom-to-be Rob, and the intention was to get him 'wasted-hammered-trashed-plastered and, in general, drunk as a skunk'. Thing was, Rob rarely drank heavily, and certainly not to the extent the guys intended for him this weekend, so he was feeling a bit uncomfortable, but also did not want to come across as a party-pooper. A round of drinks and chasers was ordered at the bar and, as soon as they were lined up, the gang grabbed the drinks and, singing boisterously, downed them in one, followed by the chasers. Rob did likewise (*as another round was ordered*) but wondered how long it would be before they were asked to leave this bar, too. So far they had been ejected from three.

As predicted in Rob's mind, after two more rounds the bartender asked them to leave because they were being too raucous – they had been asked to tone it down a couple of times already. They all left, muttering about how they would 'spend their money elsewhere'.

As they hit the windy boardwalk promenade again they headed towards the beckoning neon glow of the next bar along. They never even made it inside this time, though, as the doorman – a big, burly guy with a Mike Tyson neck – refused them entry. The same happened at the next two bars, so the guys quickly figured out they had been sussed by the 'pub-watch' network, where bars phone around to warn of potential groups of trouble coming their way. Forewarned being forearmed, so to speak. Rob did an internal shake of the head, thinking to himself he was done, and he suggested going back to the hotel and having a 'last one' in the bar there. This was met with a chorus of 'No' from the others, just as one of them noticed a 24-hour shop selling booze. They all cheered in unison as they headed off, herd-like, to the enticing lights of this 24-hour lifesaver. Rob went along with them. They came out with bagsful of the stuff.

Wondering where to drink it, they scanned the streets until, with what seemed to be a synchronous decision, opting to go and sit at the end of the pier. So off everyone went, skirting the amusement arcade and arriving at the main decking area behind it with its closed stalls, pier shops and rides, looking a little ghostly, even sinister, in the dark and with the wind blowing around them. They continued on past the dark monoliths of the rides until they found a clear-decked area at the end of the pier with some seats. A few of the group, more the worse for wear, sat gratefully on the seats. Rob sat too, with his internal dialogue telling him he really didn't want to be there anymore. He found himself taking the offered can of beer, though, popping the top, saying 'cheers' and drinking. A few began singing, while a couple of the others began to howl and whine at the moon, all their voices being carried away on the wind and out to sea.

Rob finished his beer and threw the empty can into the nearest bin. He was passed another but he shook his head, saying, 'No ... I'm done.' A few who overheard him hissed and booed as Rob repeated, 'I'm done guys, I'm off back to the hotel. Anybody coming with me?' A couple of the lads who were looking worse for wear stood as if to join him, when Dick, one of the more drunken and vocal of the group, shouted 'Pussies … losers' at them while shaking his head in disgust. It was at that precise moment that Rob 'lost it'. He stood abruptly and strode across the deck to Dick and faced him square on. 'Look, you,' said Rob, with a calm that hid his rage, making him oddly even more menacing, 'I said I'm done, and it seems so are some others. We've had some fun but I was done a while ago – but you seem to want to push and push. When will you be happy? When we get arrested for being drunk and disorderly? Or when we get turned away by the hotel? … Well, when?'

'Whoa, chill man,' said a surprised Dick, 'I'm only trying to have some fun.' 'No,' said Rob, 'you're having a go at your friends because they aren't doing what you want to do. You're bullying them and I've had enough. You're always expecting people to follow you and do what you want – well, try this: how about if *I* want you to do something? The end of the pier is there, why don't you jump off it and show us all how much fun and how daring you are? It's OK, the tides in so you'll just get wet. Go on, do that, Dick.'

'Don't be stupid,' said Dick. 'I could drown or get hurt.'

'You being a pussy then … a loser?' questioned Rob. 'Yeah, loser' came a few chants from the group.

'No,' said Dick, 'just being sensible. Jumping off a pier is dangerous and stupid.'

'And drinking till you're completely out of control isn't?' Rob asked. 'C'mon man, you lost your driving licence last year, your girlfriend the year before, and you've lost at least three jobs that I know of because you can't control your behaviour after drinking. Do you need to lose your friends too?'

The group nodded in agreement with Rob, with a few 'Yups' and 'That's rights' being blown about by the wind.

'We all like you,' reassured Rob, 'but peer pressure is just another term for bullying – and I'm guessing you really don't want people to think of you as a bully, do you?'

'No way,' said Dick, looking shocked. 'Sorry, guys,' he said looking at the group, 'I've been a bit of a penis, haven't I?

'Nah,' Rob responded, 'you've just been a bit of a Dick,' at which point the group laughed uproariously, including Dick.

'Time to go then, I guess,' Dick suggested. The group nodded and headed back towards the hotel, where they all agreed that 'one' last nightcap would suit them all very well.

WEIGHTS AND
MEASURES

Weights and Measures

This chapter is not a story but just some information, of which you may or may not be aware. 'Knowledge is power' and how we use that knowledge leads to wisdom or stupidity, control or recklessness. After obtaining this knowledge, what you choose to do with it is, well, your choice. ☺

Note
The following data is taken from the UK Government's 2010 strategy report on the effects of binge-drinking in the United Kingdom.

1. It is estimated that over 17 million working days may be lost annually due to the effects of drink-related illness, ranging from a simple hangover to more serious medical conditions.

2. The annual cost of this to employers is estimated at somewhere between £6 and £7 billion per annum.

3. The cost to the National Health Service (NHS) is in the region of £1.7 billion and rising annually.

4. Billions more are spent on the other associated clear-up operations caused by the after-effects of binge-drinking.

5. There are some 1.2 million reported incidents of alcohol-fuelled violence per year.

6. Around 40 per cent of Accident & Emergency admissions to hospital are due to alcohol-related incidents. Note that this rises to over 70 per cent between the hours of midnight and 5 a.m.

7. Approximately 150,000 people per year are hospitalized due to alcohol-related incidents.

8. It is estimated that up to 1.3 million children are affected by parents who have drink problems, and are therefore more likely to develop a drink-based problem later in life themselves.

9. Over 90 per cent of British adults consume alcohol.

10. A third of men and a fifth of women drink more than they should: men should drink no more than 21 units of alcohol per week; women should drink no more than 14 units of alcohol per week.

One unit of alcohol equals a half-pint (300ml) of beer or a small (125ml) glass of wine or a single measure of spirits.

Binge-drinking is defined as drinking more than 10 units of alcohol in one sitting for men and more than 7 units for women.

1. UK citizens spend over £30 billion on alcohol per year.

2. The UK Government raises approximately £7 billion in taxes from this.

3. Alcohol costs the UK economy over £6.4 billion in lost productivity.

4. Alcohol-fuelled crime costs £7.3 billion.

5. £4.7 billion is spent on the secondary human and emotional costs of alcohol-fuelled crime.

6. Over 22,000 people die prematurely each year due to alcohol misuse.

It is interesting to note that young, white, unemployed men are more likely to abuse alcohol.

Also worth noting is that women in skilled jobs tend to drink more heavily than other women.

Binge-drinking was once confined to the late teens, yet recent studies show it now extends from the age of 16 to 24. Some 44 per cent of people in this age bracket admit to binge-drinking on a regular basis. The Joseph Rowntree Foundation has also reported that over 50 per cent of 15- to 16-year-olds have participated at least once in binge-drinking.

Alcohol stimulates the appetite, so we are more likely to eat after a drinking session. Drinking too much also impairs our judgement, so we may not make the best choices for our post-drinking munchies. This adds other strains on the body as we become obese, which is likely to stress us into drinking more or even making us depressed, due to chemical changes in the brain caused by prolonged alcohol use. It has been shown that alcohol depletes the neurotransmitters that the brain needs to naturally prevent anxiety and depression.

Britons are the biggest binge-drinkers in Europe.

A little alcohol can boost your libido, but any more than 3 units in a day and the reverse happens. Women who drink moderately or who binge take longer to get pregnant than their more abstemious sisters.

One in 20 people in the UK admits that they cannot get through the day without a drink, and twice as many people are addicted to alcohol as to any other legal or illegal drug.

Some 88 per cent of people who drink say they could not contemplate giving up drink permanently.

Wine drinkers are less likely to get cancer than beer drinkers or those who drink spirits. This is due to *resveratrol*, a substance that is believed to inhibit cancer and is found in wine and red grape juice. Grape juice also contains three times more nitric acid than wine, which dilates the blood vessels and reduces the chances of getting a stroke.

Women who drink 2 to 5 units per day are 41 per cent more likely to develop breast cancer than women who abstain.

People who consume between 7 and 21 units of spirits (as opposed to wine) per week are twice as likely to develop cancer of the digestive tract in comparison to a tee-totaller.

These are some of the things to weigh up, and now we'll take a look at measures to take if you want to regain control.

Remember, knowledge is power, and you are now empowered to make a choice. Will you make the wise choice or the other one?

Who is truly in control?

NONE FOR
THE ROAD

None for the Road

There is an old hotel and public house in Marble Arch in London. It used to have a public gallows nearby. Prisoners found guilty and sentenced to death would be escorted to the gallows to be hanged. Prisoners were taken on a horse-drawn cart accompanied by an armed guard. As they reached the public house, it was said the armed guard would stop the cart outside and ask the prisoners if they would like 'one last drink' before they met their fate. If the prisoners said yes they were given 'one for the road'; if they declined, then they remained 'on the wagon'.

Tim entered the bar and immediately spotted his friends. He noted unconsciously that he'd actually heard them a micro-second before he saw them. They had been friends since university, and were still as raucous now as they ever were in their student days. They then saw him and waved him over. As he got within speaking distance he heard Chris, one of his friends, declare, 'My round. What's everyone having?' People placed their orders, with Tim requesting a large tonic water with ice and lemon. Once everyone had their drinks and after the appropriate 'cheers' ritual had been gone through, Owen, another of the foursome of friends, questioned, 'Still on the wagon, then, Tim?'

'During the week, yes,' said Tim. 'I'm not tee-total, though; I still have a drink at the weekends.'

'How come?' chipped in Jon. 'Why the midweek abstinence?'

'I kind of needed to,' Tim replied. 'I kept turning up for work late, and in a bit of a bad state. Luckily my boss is a carrot-rather-than-stick type, but I think one day I pushed it a bit far and he called me into his office.'

The other three shook their heads in unison and muttered 'uh-oh.'

'Tore a strip off?' asked Chris.

'Not really,' Tim continued. 'He asked me what was wrong and whether he could help. I replied there was nothing wrong, to which he then asked why I was doing all the boozing and coming to work hung over and why was I putting in jeopardy a very promising future. I remember shaking my head, feeling a bit like a little boy in front of the headmaster for claiming his dog had eaten his homework … again.'

They all laughed, remembering similar instances in their own lives.

Tim carried on, 'Then he asked me what the drink did for me, to which I answered, "It relaxes me, I guess." And he pressed on with, "So what's causing you to be stressed?" followed by, "work, money, relationships, or is it something else?" "All of those to some degree," I answered, "well, actually not work; I like my job," I added hastily, and I remember him nodding gently and kind of reminding me of Yoda when he grew impatient with Luke Skywalker.' Tim's friends all cracked up at this, as each formed an image in mind of this encounter. 'Not strong with you is the force, young Tim,' said Chris in a mock Yoda-ish voice. They all laughed even more.

Tim went on, 'What he said next, though, really surprised

me in the simplicity of its wisdom.' The other three looked on with faces that demanded more information.

'Well, my boss pointed out to me that the drink was costing me money, and thus made my money situation worse, and if it continued I could drink myself out of a good job that I liked and make it even worse still. He then pointed out he recalled I'd had a nice girlfriend until a few months ago, and that she'd dumped me because I preferred to go out and have a drink than be with her. He then also added that if I was out looking for a girlfriend, would I be actively looking for a woman who got drunk all the time and could embarrass me?'

The group was silent as Tim said, 'Basically I guess he kind of had me nailed on the problem front, but what I needed was a solution.' Tim's face broke into a grin before he continued, 'And you know what? The wise old codger gave me one.'

'OK, now you have us all curious,' Owen declared.

'Well,' said Tim, 'He told me about his brother, who'd had a major drink issue to the point where he lost his business due to making some bad decisions, and lost his family when his wife left him. His brother finally got some help and my boss was going to show me some of the stuff his brother had been taught.' Tim paused and took a drink of tonic before adding, 'You see, my boss said he liked me and thought I had a good future and could do well in the company, but only if I had a clear head, and I apparently had not had that at work for a while, hence our "chat". My boss didn't want to see me head down the same route as his brother and wanted to highlight to me some choices I could make about my future and give me some tools to use.' Tim frowned. 'I think he struck a chord because I realized I was on a bit of a slippery slope, and wasn't capable of putting on the brakes without some help, and here it seemed to be, so I was all ears.'

'A bit like Yoda,' Chris joked, ever the comedian of the group. They all laughed before Jon said, 'Go on.'

'OK,' Tim continued. 'He told me that his brother, after everything had gone wrong, decided to get some help and was referred to this "top dude" in Harley Street, a therapist or coach or something, and apparently after working with him just the once he came away a changed man.'

'Changed how?' enquired Jon.

'Changed in that he had learned how to control his stress and anxiety, and in turn his drinking,' replied Tim.

'My boss said his brother learned a few techniques in this session, but there was one that stood out over the others in both how easy it is to use and how effective it is. My boss' brother taught him it, and he taught it to me, and it's what I have been using ever since, and … you know what? It works.'

'Cool,' said Chris. 'How does it work, then?'

'Really well,' replied Tim with a smile. 'Well, it does for me, anyway.'

'Jesus, it's like pulling teeth,' said Owen. 'Tell us what it is already.'

'Why do you want to know?' asked Tim with a teasing grin.

'Because it sounds like it may be useful,' said Owen, while Jon and Chris nodded in agreement.

'Oh, it *is* useful,' said Tim, 'but only if you use it; otherwise it is use-less.'

'Well, show us and we'll find out then, won't we?' cried Owen in mock frustration. Tim threw up his hands in submission. 'OK, here goes. Copy me.'

They all nodded in agreement, Chris adding, 'Yes, Obi-wan' on behalf of the group. They all giggled like 10-year-olds.

'Copy me,' Tim repeated. 'Take your index finger and find the outside edge of the eye socket bone, then rub down and along the bone until you find a dip in the bone, kind of a "V" or "U" shape … got it?' They all nodded to confirm they had.

'Good, now put your second finger next to the first so you have a finger tip each side of the dip in the bone.' Tim looked at them all to check they were in the right place. Happy that they were, he continued, 'OK, now lightly trace a little circle inwards with a little bit of pressure for about ten or so circles, then stop and do the same thing in the opposite direction.'

'Good, then go back again but this time press really hard so it's almost painful, again for about ten circles, then finally go back the other way but this time take all the pressure off so you are just gently stroking the surface of the skin … cool, then take your fingers away.' They all did so as Tim enquired, 'So how does your head feel now?'

'All light, kind of floaty,' said Jon.

'Yeah,' agreed Owen. 'Nice. A bit spacey.'

'Bit like having a spliff,' Chris said – 'not that I'd know,' he feigned mock seriousness, 'just what I imagine it would be like.' They all laughed before saying in unison, 'Yeah, right.'

'Right, then,' said Tim, 'let me ask you … try to think of something stressful right now.' They all looked at each other with a mixture of confusion, surprise and delight before Jon said, 'I can't! Well, it seems like if I tried I could, but I really don't feel like it at all.'

'Yes,' echoed Chris and Owen, 'that's exactly it … Wow, cool.'

'Yup, cool,' agreed Tim. 'And that's it, that's all I have to do. I don't need a drink to unwind from being wound up, I simply do this eye-rub technique, and I chill in a nanosecond. I'm also spending less and feeling much better at work, and another thing that's surprised me is that when I *do* have a drink at the weekend, I really, really enjoy it now.'

'And that's all you have been doing?' asked Chris. 'Yup, just that,' Tim responded with a firm nod. He then followed by saying, 'Oh, you may have noticed I have not left to go out for a smoke, either. I quit smoking last week by using this. Every time I felt like a ciggie I stopped and did the eye rub, and then found I didn't need a cigarette after all. I'm gonna save a fortune at this rate. Oh and my boss is much happier with the way I'm performing now so I may be due for a promotion review soon, so all's well that ends well, it seems.'

'So what's it like just drinking tonic water, then?' asked Jon.

'Bit like drinking vodka and tonic but without the vodka,' Chris quipped.

'Exactly that,' confirmed Tim with a smile. 'Think I might try one, too,' said Owen. 'Me, too,' agreed Jon. 'And me, but with an eye-rub chaser,' Chris said.

They all started to rub frantically around their eyes with manically exaggerated gestures before falling about laughing as Jon went to the bar to get the drinks.

SLEEP WELL

Sleep Well

'Some people see the glass half full.
Others see it half empty. I see a glass
that's twice as big as it needs to be.'
– George Carlin

Gill sat in the window seat of the new bistro in the small town where she lived. She'd chosen the window so she could look out to see her friend arrive, as she was worried she might miss her, or that her friend, Kate, might miss the bistro.

This was Gill all over: if there were something to worry about, she could and would. She had a Black Belt in her ability to catastrophize. She even worried about having nothing to worry about, and spoke of the 'calm before the storm', etc. All of her friends and family had learned that they must never say two specific words to Gill … those words were *Don't worry*.

She picked up her phone and logged on to the news app on it and sat there shaking her head as she went from one bad news story to another. As she was flicking over to another app with more news, she did not notice Kate sitting down next to her. 'That bad, is it?' Kate asked as she took her seat. 'Oh, where did you come from?' smiled Gill. 'I've been looking out for you.'

'Must have slipped in while you were in deep trance with your phone,' replied Kate, adding, 'So, have you been here long?'

'Oh, just 5 minutes or so,' said Gill, 'not even had chance to order a drink yet, so no, not that long.'

'Well, what shall we have, then?' Kate asked. 'I quite fancy a glass of wine if that's OK with you?' She then asked, 'Are we eating, too?'

'Food would be good,' remarked Gill, picking up the menu and looking it over. 'You haven't been here since it's been revamped, have you?' she asked.

'No,' said Kate, looking around, 'they've done a very nice job, though. It feels very cosy and inviting.'

'Well, I'm sticking to fish tonight, so are we OK having a white wine – if we *are* having a bottle?' Gill asked, 'Or I can have it by the glass if you'd prefer red,' she followed quickly, sounding almost apologetic.

'White's fine,' said Kate. 'They have a very nice Gavi, which will go with your fish and the chicken I'm having, so that's that done.'

'Wish I could be so assured and decisive,' remarked Gill. 'I could have spent half an hour on that wine list and then ended up telling you to choose.' She laughed, but it was not a happy laugh, Kate noted.

Kate reached out and touched the back of her friend's hand as she asked, 'Are you OK, hon? … You seem perturbed?'

'Just the usual,' Gill sighed. 'Work's busy and a bit stressy, then I go home, rustle up some food and have a couple of glasses of wine, watch some TV then go to bed, and then find I can't sleep so I have a brandy to see if that helps … it doesn't. I guess I eventually nod off because I wake up, but I never feel refreshed, always groggy. Then it's another day of same old, same old.'

'Aw, Gill, you sound really down.'

'I am,' confirmed Gill, 'I'm sick and tired of feeling sick and tired, especially the tired bit. My mind just won't rest, not even when I go to bed or even if I try to make it relaxed with a drink.' Gill caught herself and added, 'Sorry, hon, I'm whining when we should be, er, wining and dining.'

''s OK,' Kate reassured her. 'I may just have a few tricks that may help you with this, but first let's order.' Kate beckoned over the waitress, who duly took their order and returned promptly with the wine. Kate sampled it and gave a nod, allowing the waitress to pour them both a glass. Gill sipped hers and gave a complimentary nod. 'Nice choice,' she declared, 'this is lovely.'

'I know, I get it from the supermarket sometimes, though at a third of this price,' Kate said with mild annoyance. 'Guess we're paying for the ambience!'

Gill laughed, 'Indeed. And the company's good, too! It's great to see you, and I'm sorry to have begun the evening moaning.'

'Not at all,' Kate said. 'That's what friends are for ... anyway, there must be some reason as I have recently learned some very interesting, not to mention amazing, relaxation techniques from a friend of mine who teaches yoga and does some therapy stuff, too. I think it might really help you sleep. I know it's helped me.'

'I didn't know you had a problem sleeping, Kate,' said Gill in surprise.

'I don't normally,' Kate responded, 'but since the takeover at work things have changed, and not always for the better, and some of the new procedures and projects are a little stretching, to say the least, meaning I am still working in my head as I try to get to sleep at night. Very frustrating, especially as I'm not getting paid for it!' she laughed. 'Not any more, though,' she added triumphantly. 'Suzy has taught me some very cool things to overcome this issue ... and now I sleep like a baby.'

'Really?' Gill said, looking surprised. 'Can you show them to me ... please?'

'Of course,' Kate assured her. 'Told you I was here for a reason tonight.'

At that moment the waitress bought their starter dishes and Kate insisted they put all discussion of relaxation techniques on hold until she had eaten her crab cakes with sashimi sauce, as she was, as she put it, 'a zillion per cent ravenous'. Gill agreed and confirmed that she was just as hungry … well, maybe only a billion per cent, not a zillion. They both laughed and quietly ate their food. As they finished, the eagle-eyed waitress took away their plates, asking if all was 'OK?'

They both nodded an agreed 'Yes' and the waitress smiled and took the plates to the kitchen.

'So, is it complicated, this stuff you have learned?' enquired Gill. 'No, not really. Once you've done it a few times it's relatively simple. The hardest thing is making it into a habit,' said Kate. 'It's mostly about breathing and some acupuncture stuff.'

Gill looked horrified. 'No, No,' she said, 'I can't do needles.'

Kate laughed, 'No needles, just touching some acupuncture points with your fingertips and breathing.' Then reaffirming the 'No needles, I promise,' Gill gave a 'Phew' as she dramatically wiped her brow with her napkin. 'So what does it involve, then?' she asked again.

'OK,' said Kate, 'easiest thing to do is *just do it*, so copy me … mirror what I do.' With that, Kate straightened up in her chair. Gill did likewise.

'Now do this exercise with me,' Kate said.

'Touch each of the following points with two fingers, breathing in through your nose and out through your mouth slowly,' instructed Kate:

- *Top of head on the crown*

- *Above your eye at the inner end of your eyebrow above your nose*

- *Outside edge of your eye*

- *Under your eye (top of your cheekbone)*

- *Above your top lip and under your bottom lip*

- *Under your collarbones at the inner end under your neck*

- *Under your arms, 4 inches down the side of your body*

- *Middle of your forehead between your eyebrows and about half an inch up (breathe three times on this spot).*

'OK,' Kate said, '… that's it for that bit. How do you feel?'

'Wow,' exclaimed Gill, 'like I've been meditating or in a sauna for half an hour. That's amazing. How does it work?'

'Very well, apparently,' smirked Kate.

At that moment the waitress arrived with the baked sea bass and chicken supreme, and placing them down in front of the women. 'Hope you enjoy,' said the waitress. Both women just gave her a kind of goofy smile and said 'Thank you.' The waitress turned away and headed to her station with a mildly furrowed brow.

Kate and Gill had a very quiet conversation as they ate, discussing nothing of any urgency or importance, just enjoying each other's company.

As both women finished their meal at pretty much the same time, Gill said, 'I really like it here. This place makes you feel very relaxed. I haven't felt so chilled out for a long time.' Kate gave her a knowing smile as she responded, 'The place *may* have something to do with it, but the breathing technique played a big part, too.' 'You think?' asked Gill.

'I *know*,' Kate replied.

'Well, I feel really mellow at the moment, so is there anything else to know?' asked Gill.

'Indeed there is, my friend' Kate answered. 'I noted a couple of things you said earlier about coping with stress with a couple of glasses of wine when you got home, and then having a brandy to help you sleep. I have to tell you that's not going to work in either case. If work stress is an issue you have to deal with it at source, not react to it later in your "own" time, because that's time you "own" and it belongs to you, not your employer. Self-medicating over stress by using any drug, legal or illegal, does not remove the stress. All you do is get into a bad habit of becoming reliant on the drug of choice to help you get through stressy times, and that really isn't healthy. If you need to relax and take your mind off things, just do the relaxation breathing technique I taught you.'

'I'll never remember it,' said Gill.

'You don't need to,' Kate said. 'I'll email it to you along with the other things I want to show you.'

'Thank you,' Gill said, softly. 'So what else is there to learn, oh wise one?' she continued as she pressed her palms together in front of her forehead and gave a small bow. Kate poured them the remains of the wine from the bottle as she said, 'Well, there is another breathing technique called "collarbone breathing". I use it every morning and it makes me feel great. It prevents negative thoughts from developing and also kickstarts and energizes the meridian system, while at the same time being very relaxing, but not in a makes-you-sleepy kind of way.'

'Sounds great,' Gill said enthusiastically. 'Especially the bit about stopping negative thoughts, which I could really do with. I know I have a real "Murphy's law" mentality and I wish I could stop it and see more positivity in the world.'

'OK, then,' Kate said, sitting more upright in her chair again. 'Copy me as I do this, then.'

Gill mirrored Kate as Kate did the following:

'First, find the "knuckle" on the inner end of your collarbone, just where it joins the top of the breastbone. There's one on each side. Then drop your fingers down about an inch, to the first soft space above your first rib. That's the collarbone point. OK, now place the fingertips of one of your hands, either one as you're going to do both anyway, and, once you have your fingertips there, begin to tap the back of that hand with the fingertips of your other hand, between the little finger and the ring finger knuckle. Continue to tap as you do this breathing pattern:

- *Take a deep breath in and hold it for a couple of seconds*

- *Release half the breath and hold for a couple of seconds*

- *Release all the breath and hold for a couple of seconds*

- *Take in half a breath and hold it for a couple of seconds*

- *Then breathe normally.*

'Now fold your fingers and put your top knuckles where the fingertips were and, making sure your thumb does not make any contact with your skin, tap the same spot on the back of your hand and repeat the breathing exercise as you continue to tap. Then, once that has been done, move the knuckles of the same hand across to the other collarbone point and tap as you do the breathing cycle. Once that is completed, open your hand so your fingertips are now touching the collarbone point and repeat the tapping and the breathing cycle again.

'That's one half of the exercise done. Now repeat it on the other hand, using exactly the same hand positions, tapping and breathing till the exercise is complete.'

Once both Kate and Gill had completed the exercise, Kate asked, 'How do you feel now?'

'Really relaxed, a bit spacey, but kind of energized, too,' Gill responded.

'Try thinking of something negative now and getting bothered by it,' suggested Kate.

Gill scanned the room and then laughed as she said, 'I can't, like I don't care, sort of? It's like I can't be bothered to be bothered about being bothered.'

Kate laughed out loud. 'What a great way to put it! That's exactly it. I actually call it the "Carriage Clock" exercise. You know those old-fashioned clocks with the glass dome over them? It's like this exercise puts a glass dome, a kind of bubble of calm, around you. You can see out at everything you need to see, but if negative stuff tries to get to you it just hits the glass and gets repelled, bounces off. It just can't get to you.'

'Perfect way to describe it,' agreed Gill. 'I've been trying to think of negative issues but just can't be bothered. Wow; I have my own bubble of calm!'

'Well, I do the collarbone breathing every morning,' Kate said, 'in an almost ritual manner. It only takes 2 minutes and it gets me focused, and I just seem to have a better day as a result. Not much gets to me now, and if anything is really overwhelming I can always re-do the collarbone breathing and it seems to do the trick. Bottom line is *I am back in control.*'

'I like both of those techniques,' said Gill. 'But ... what if you need an instant fix? I know they both take only a couple of minutes, but what if you get a sudden "overwhelm"?'

'Well,' Kate responded, 'I always try to excuse myself for the couple of minutes I need to do the collarbone or relaxation breathing by saying I need the bathroom – but if I were ever someplace I couldn't do that, then there's always the reverse breathing technique. That's supposed to help, though I have never tried it. Shall we give it a go now?'

'OK, let's,' smiled Gill.

Kate continued, 'OK imagine a panicky situation where you may get flustered, then do the following:

'Reverse your breathing – that is, breathe in through your mouth quite forcefully, and then out through your nose, again quite forcefully, and again and again so we do it three times in total.'

Both women completed the exercise and then fell into hysterics as Gill said, 'That sounded like Darth Vader having an asthma attack.' Kate roared with laughter and then, as she calmed down, said, 'I know, but it does stop the anxiety – and maybe the breathing can be done with a little more subtlety than we just did it?'

'I'm sure,' agreed Gill. 'I'll feed back to you when I have tried it out in the real world.' 'Me too,' laughed Kate. 'You having dessert?' she enquired.

'You know, usually I would – but I don't feel the need now. I think I'm just going to have a nice latte to finish the evening before I go home and re-do the breathing before bed. And, you know,' Gill added, affecting an upper-class accent, 'I'll save a *fortune* on brandy, darling, as I only like the good stuff.'

Kate smiled and said, 'Latte for me, too, I think, and ditto with the breathing before bed.'

The women ordered their coffees and drank them as they carried on discussing a film they'd been to see the week before, and the book Kate was reading with her bookgroup. When the bill came Gill grabbed it and said, 'This is on me and no arguments. Tonight has been lovely – not only seeing you and having a nice meal but also very valuable with the things you have shown me. I get a good feeling now that I will be able to take back control, so thank you.'

'Thank you for inviting me, and I am glad to help. We must do this again soon.'

'Deal,' agreed Gill as she paid the bill. They stood up and both thanked the waitress. The waitress thought there must have been something in the food, because both women looked 'different' from when they'd come in, one of them especially, and they had only had one bottle of wine between them, so surely it couldn't have been that. They both looked very calm yet controlled at the same time. 'I need to calm down a little myself,' thought the waitress as she rushed to clear their table.

BACK IN CONTROL

Back in Control!

Now you've read the stories about how these
techniques can help, here are the practical step-
by-step instructions to put you back in control:

Meridian Tapping
Techniques for dealing with:

- cravings/addictions
- stress
- trauma
- anger and frustration
- guilt and shame
- pain
- feeling 'down'

Is What I'm Drinking OK for Me to Drink?

- the Yes/No Technique
- the Smooth/Sticky Technique

Just the Tonic

Negativity and How to Stay Out of It

- reversal techniques
- collarbone breathing
- reverse breathing

Anchoring

- creating positive anchors
- collapsing negative anchors

Positive Imagery

Relaxation Breathing

Eye Relaxation Rub

Meridian Tapping

Meridian techniques, first discovered by Dr Roger Callahan, are a rapid and powerful way to take the sting out of negative emotional states. If we drink too much as a form of self-medication because we feel anxious, stressed, down or in some other kind of mental (or even physical) pain, then logic must say that if we remove the negative state, we will no longer need to self-medicate. It is a simple cause-and-effect paradigm. If the cause is no longer there then the need to take the action (in this case drinking too much) is removed as well.

Meridian techniques, whether TFT (Thought Field Therapy) or EFT (Emotional Freedom Techniques), have been shown time and time again to bring rapid relief to a host of sufferers. What I like about these techniques is that they are rapid and require no belief in them for them to work. I have treated many a sceptic with TFT and witnessed a mixture of confusion and delight when they realize the issue they came to me about is no longer there. My favourite words in Meridian Therapy are: 'It's gone!'

The following sequences are just a few from a multitude of possibilities, which can enable you to collapse negative states and allow you to have the freedom to make wiser choices in how you deal with alcohol and many other substances.

Cravings/Addictions

Cravings and addictions are the subconscious mind's way of letting you know you have a stress or anxiety that is becoming overwhelming and needs anaesthetizing or blocking – hence turning to drink or other drugs to get 'out of your mind'. Using the following sequences you can make these anxieties and stressors collapse, quickly, easily and with no damaging side-effects.

Anxieties can be complex and of course are different for each individual; that is why we have three possible sequences. Try one and if it does not work, then try the next.

The PR Triangle

Always do the Psychological Reversal (PR) Triangle prior to doing any sequence. (For more about PR, see page 129.) The PR Triangle is as follows:

- **Tap (karate chop) on the side of your hand, point and say:**

    'I want to be ...' (in control/fit/healthy or whatever you choose to say)

    'I can be ...'

    'I will be ...'

    'I am ...'

    'I'm OK.'

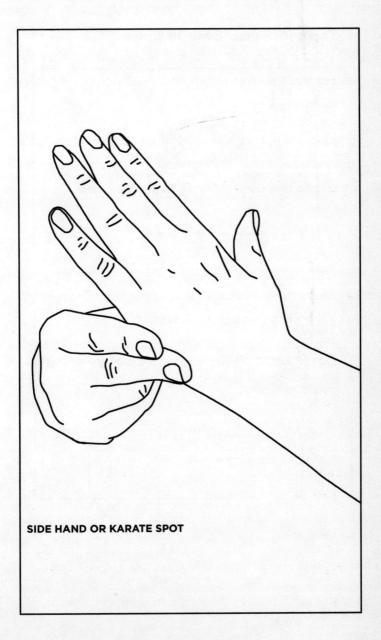

SIDE HAND OR KARATE SPOT

- **Tap under your nose 30 times**

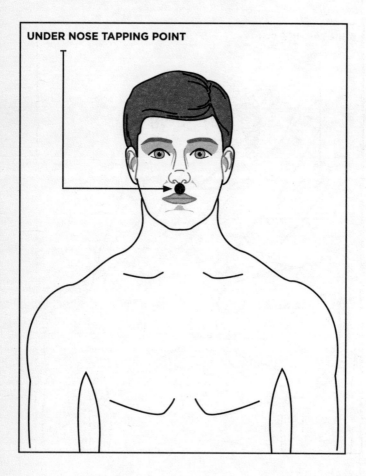

UNDER NOSE TAPPING POINT

- **Tap your chin 30 times**

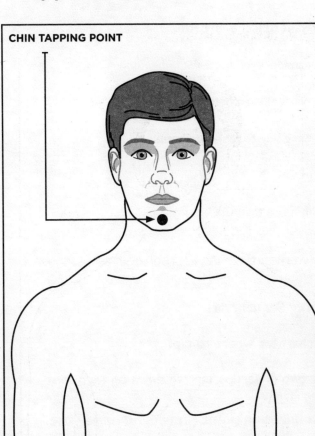

CHIN TAPPING POINT

- **Tap your other hand and say:**

  'I want to feel even better.'

  'I can feel even better.'

  'I will feel even better.'

  'I am going to feel even better.'

  'I'm OK.'

  'I'm more than OK.'

Then work through the appropriate craving sequence.

Craving Sequence 1

(See chart for where to tap)

Using two fingertips, tap ten times on each spot:

- **Collarbone point (inner end under the 'knuckle')**

- **Under the eye**

- **Collarbone point (inner end under the 'knuckle')**

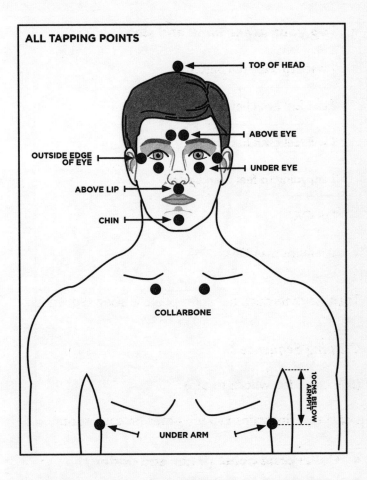

ALL TAPPING POINTS

TOP OF HEAD

ABOVE EYE

OUTSIDE EDGE OF EYE

UNDER EYE

ABOVE LIP

CHIN

COLLARBONE

10CMS BELOW ARMPIT

UNDER ARM

- **Tap the back of your hand by your little finger knuckle continuously**

- **Close your eyes**

- **Open your eyes**

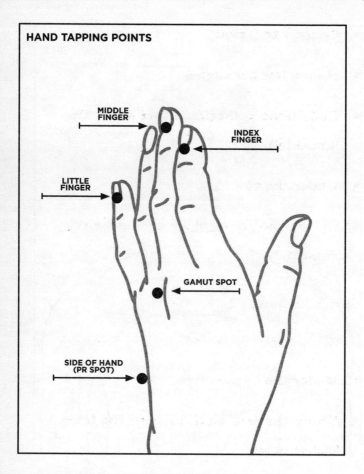

HAND TAPPING POINTS

- **Look down to the left**

- **Look down to the right**

- **Roll your eyes one way, then the other**

- **Hum a few bars of 'Happy Birthday'**

- **Count 1 to 5 aloud**

- **Hum a few bars again**

- **Collarbone point (inner end under the 'knuckle')**

- **Under the eye**

- **Collarbone point (inner end under the 'knuckle')**

Craving Sequence 2

Using two fingertips, tap ten times on each spot:

- **Under the eye**

- **Under the arm on the side of the body 4 inches down**

- **Collarbone point (inner end under the 'knuckle')**

- **Tap the back of your hand by your little finger knuckle continuously**

- **Close your eyes**

- **Open your eyes**

- **Look down to the left**

- **Look down to the right**

- **Roll your eyes one way, then the other**

- **Hum a few bars of 'Happy Birthday'**

- **Count 1 to 5 aloud**

- **Hum a few bars again**

- **Under the eye**

- **Under the arm on the side of the body 4 inches down**

- **Collarbone point (inner end under the 'knuckle')**

Craving Sequence 3

Using two fingertips, tap ten times on each spot:

- **Under the eye**

- **Collarbone point (inner end under the 'knuckle')**

- **Under the arm on the side of the body 4 inches down**

- **Collarbone point (inner end under the 'knuckle')**

- **Tap the back of your hand by your little finger knuckle continuously**

- **Close your eyes**

- **Open your eyes**

- **Look down to the left**

- **Look down to the right**

- **Roll your eyes one way, then the other**

- **Hum a few bars of 'Happy Birthday'**

- **Count 1 to 5 aloud**

- **Hum a few bars again**

- **Under the eye**

- **Collarbone point (inner end under the 'knuckle')**

- **Under the arm on the side of the body 4 inches down**

- **Collarbone point (inner end under the 'knuckle')**

One of these sequences should enable you to collapse the 'sudden' urge to take a drink and/or to help you get out of a negative state of stress, anxiety, sadness or pain.

Note

This is not meant to put you off drinking or stop you drinking but is a tool to enable you to have more control and to not 'have to' turn to drink to control your emotions.

Dealing with Stress

Modern life, whether it be work-based or family, has a tendency to create an inordinate amount of stress, and once again it is very easy to turn to a legal drug like alcohol to anaesthetize ourselves. We can often feel trapped or out of control in our lives. It does seem odd to me that that's when we turn to imbibe something that actually makes us less in control. So why not try this instead next time you are feeling stressed out?

First tap the PR sequence (as shown on page 94).

Using two fingertips, tap six times on each spot:

- **Under the eye**

- **Under the arm on the side of the body 4 inches down**

- **Under the eye**

- **Collarbone point (inner end under the 'knuckle')**

- **Tap the back of your hand by your little finger knuckle continuously**

- **Close your eyes**

- **Open your eyes**

- **Look down to the left**

- **Look down to the right**

- **Roll your eyes one way, then the other**

- **Hum a few bars of 'Happy Birthday'**

- **Count 1 to 5 aloud**

- **Hum a few bars again**

- **Under the eye**

- **Under the arm on the side of the body 4 inches down**

- **Under the eye**

- **Collarbone point (inner end under the 'knuckle')**

If at any point the feelings fail to fall away, this may be a result of what's known as PR, or Psychological Reversal (for more about this, see page 129). To correct for this, tap the side of your hand (karate chop point) six to ten times. Then start again.

This sequence only takes a minute to do (probably quicker than finding a bottle of wine and opening it), so if you are feeling stressed or pressured use this simple technique to enable yourself to take back some control so you can enjoy having a drink for the right reasons.

Dealing with Trauma

Bad stuff happens in life and many people turn to alcohol or other drugs to numb the pain of the memories of the 'bad stuff'. Sadly this only temporarily numbs the pain and so we learn to drink more often or even stay almost permanently drunk to enable us to cope. You can see this written on the face of any drunken homeless person you encounter, or see it in the eyes of, for example, a former soldier suffering from PTSD (Post Traumatic Stress Disorder). It is no coincidence, I believe, that many of the homeless walking the streets are former servicemen and -women using alcohol to cope with the pain of the memories they hold.

Meridian Therapy has been used widely in areas of high trauma such as Kosovo and Rwanda and in post-Hurricane Katrina disaster areas to great effect, and has brought about life-changing results in these areas. In fact, in Kosovo the effect was so great the Chief Medical Officer of the sitting government made a statement that TFT Meridian Therapy was to be the first-choice intervention in dealing with PTSD.

If you have experienced a traumatic incident, try the following sequence and see if it alleviates the situation.

Trauma

Once again, tap the PR sequence as shown on page 94.

Using two fingertips, tap six times on each point:

- **Above the eye on the inner end of the eyebrow**

- **Under the eye**

- **Under the arm**

- **Collarbone**

- **End of index finger (on outside edge by the nail)**

- **Collarbone**

- **End of little finger (on inside edge by the nail)**

- **Collarbone**

- **Tap the back of your hand by your little finger knuckle continuously**

- **Close your eyes**

- **Open your eyes**

- **Look down to the left**

- **Look down to the right**

- **Roll your eyes one way, then the other**

- **Hum a few bars of 'Happy Birthday'**

- **Count 1 to 5 aloud**

- **Hum a few bars again**

Then tap again the first part of the sequence:

- **Above the eye on the inner end of the eyebrow**

- **Under the eye**

- **Under the arm**

- **Collarbone**

- **End of index finger (on outside edge by the nail)**

- **Collarbone**

- **End of little finger (on inside edge by the nail)**

- **Collarbone**

- **Tap the back of your hand by your little finger knuckle continuously**

- **Using your eyes only, look at the floor and roll your eyes directly up to the ceiling**

If at any point the feelings fail to fall away, this may be a result of what's known as PR, or Psychological Reversal (for more about this, see page 129). To correct for this, tap the side of your hand (karate chop point) six to ten times. Then start again at the beginning.

You can use this sequence to overcome all types of trauma including accidents, grief, bereavement, violence and many other trauma-inducing issues.

Dealing with Anger and Frustration

A close cohort of stress is anger and/or frustration. We feel helpless, and this helplessness can make us get 'wound up'. So what do we do? We feel we need to 'unwind', and we do this by getting drunk. Oddly, though, the anger and frustration do not go away and we can sometimes, in our new drunken state, vent this anger by being abusive or even violent … kind of 'punch drunk', if you like. The consequences of this behaviour are not good, and certainly in the long term do you no good … especially if the long term is a jail term.

So if you begin to become aware that you are getting 'wound up', simply tap the following sequence.

Tap the PR sequence at the start of this section (page 94).

Then tap the following points using the first two fingers, about six times per point:

- **End of the little finger (on inside edge by the nail)**

- **Inside the middle finger**

- **Collarbone**

- **Tap the back of your hand by your little finger knuckle continuously**

- **Close your eyes**

- **Open your eyes**

- **Look down to the left**

- **Look down to the right**

- **Roll your eyes one way, then the other**

- **Hum a few bars of 'Happy Birthday'**

- **Count 1 to 5 aloud**

- **Hum a few bars again**

- **End of little finger (on inside edge by the nail)**

- **Inside the middle finger**

- **Collarbone**

Quite often just tapping the first part of this sequence is enough to take you from a DefCon 2 alarm state to being calm again.

I also noticed while observing a client who had major anger issues that after I had taught them to tap this, they naturally, when getting angry, just pressed down on the end of their little finger as if they were stretching or distorting the meridian. I have since tried this with many clients, all of whom find that if they stretch the meridian by pushing down on the end of their little finger they are not able to access the emotion of anger. *(This latter part is currently an experimental technique and not validated other than by anecdotal evidence; however, try it. It can do no harm and may just work for you, too.)*

Dealing with Guilt and Shame

Another set of pernicious emotions are the two
bedfellows of guilt and shame. We can do something bad
and feel guilt or shame, or sometimes *not* do something
and feel guilty and ashamed. Once again it is very easy
to attempt to anaesthetize or lessen these unwelcome
feelings by losing ourselves in a bottle. Problem is we then
feel even more guilty and ashamed, and thus we end up
in this loop or spiral, from which there seems no escape.
Guilt is also often a side-effect of PTSD and in some cases
is the major emotional trigger.

If you experience any of this, tap the following:

Tap the PR sequence described at the start of this
section (page 94).

Then tap the following points, using the first two fingers
of either hand, about six times per point:

- **End of the index finger (on the outside edge
  by the nail)**

- **Collarbone**

- **On the chin point under your bottom lip**

- **Collarbone**

- **Tap the back of your hand by your little finger knuckle continuously**

- **Close your eyes**

- **Open your eyes**

- **Look down to the left**

- **Look down to the right**

- **Roll your eyes one way, then the other**

- **Hum a few bars of 'Happy Birthday'**

- **Count 1 to 5 aloud**

- **Hum a few bars again**

- **End of the index finger (on the outside edge by the nail)**

- **Collarbone**

- **On the chin point under the bottom lip**

- **Collarbone**

Carrying guilt and shame is like carrying a bag full of rubbish around with you. The above sequence will enable you to put down the bag and leave it behind.

Dealing with Pain

Pain can be emotional or physical, or sometimes both. John Sarno, an American MD, posits the theory that most back, neck and shoulder pain is related to trapped stress and anger. No matter the cause, the result is, again, often dealt with by prescribed medication, which we sometimes reinforce with non-prescribed self-medication to help us through the day. I have seen in many clients that, once you remove the emotional cause, the physical manifestation of pain vanishes, too.

It should be noted that it is wise to have a full check-up done by a physician when dealing with pain to rule out anything obvious that may be causing the pain to persist. Once this has been done, then you can try the following sequence to see how your experience of pain may change.

Meridian Therapy will only remove or alleviate inappropriate pain and not 'appropriate' pain, so if pain persists after the tapping then there may be other areas to investigate. For this you should see both your physician and also consult, where possible, a qualified Meridian therapist.

Focus on your pain now and tap the following:

- **Tap the PR sequence described at the start of this section (see page 94).**

- **Tap the spot between your little finger and the ring finger knuckle on the back of your hand 50 times**

- **Tap the collarbone point 10 times**

- **Tap the back of your hand by your little finger knuckle continuously**

- **Close your eyes**

- **Open your eyes**

- **Look down to the left**

- **Look down to the right**

- **Roll your eyes one way, then the other**

- **Hum a few bars of 'Happy Birthday'**

- **Count I to 5 aloud**

- **Hum a few bars again**

- **Tap the spot between your little finger and the ring finger knuckle on the back of your hand 50 times**

- **Tap the collarbone point 10 times.**

Re-evaluate how the pain feels now and, if needed, repeat the sequence as and when required.

Note
This sequence will not help with the pain of a hangover (I know, I've tried it!). Mother Nature did not give us any help on that score. ☹

Dealing with Feeling 'Down'

Some days we wake and feel like we are going to have a bad day, and to be honest that's OK, however what we need to do is ask ourselves who is giving us this crap? As I said earlier, who is it who walks into your room in the morning and says 'OK, here it is … this is the box of crap you have to carry around all day … enjoy'?

Truth is, we do it to ourselves … *we* decide how our day is going to be.

OK, that said, some of us have got into the habit of having most, if not all, of our days be crappy ones, and again this is stressful and painful in its own way, so again we self-medicate. Is cider and cornflakes the answer? I don't know … but you can try this alternative:

Tap the PR sequence at the start of this section (page 94), and make sure you use positive affirmations such as:

> *'I want to feel good for no reason at all.'*

> *'I can feel good for no reason at all.'*

> *'I will feel good for no reason at all.'*

> *'I am feeling good.'*

> *'I'm OK – I'm more than OK.'*

Then tap the following, using two fingertips, six times on each point:

- **Above the eye on the inner end of the eyebrow**
- **Under the eye**

- **Under the arm**

- **Under the eye**

- **Under the nose**

- **Tap the spot between your little finger and ring finger knuckle on the back of your hand 50 times**

- **Tap the collarbone point 10 times**

- **Tap the back of your hand by your little finger knuckle continuously**

- **Close your eyes**

- **Open your eyes**

- **Look down to the left**

- **Look down to the right**

- **Roll your eyes one way, then the other**

- **Hum a few bars of 'Happy Birthday'**

- **Count I to 5 aloud**

- **Hum a few bars again**

- **Tap above the eye on the inner end of the eyebrow**

- **Under the eye**

- **Under the arm**

- **Under the eye**

- **Under the nose**

- **Tap the spot between your little finger and the ring finger knuckle on the back of your hand 50 times**

- **Tap the collarbone point 10 times**

Re-evaluate how you feel now.

How often or how easily can you feel bad for no reason? Ask yourself … why would you choose to do that? Now you have some simple to use strategies, would you ever choose to feel that way again? Answers on a postcard and mail them to your good self, please …

Is What I'm Drinking OK for Me to Drink?

How do you know if what you are drinking is harming you?

The Yes/No Technique

Also known as the 'Jekyll and Hyde' test, as explained in my previous book *Positive Shrinking*, this is a technique that lets you know if what you ingest or inhale is OK for you or not. I am repeating this powerful exercise here. The belief is based on the idea that the body has an intrinsic sense or intelligence about what is OK, or not, for it. The technique uses a form of internal kinesiology where you ask yourself 'Is something OK for me right now?' Your body will give you a 'yes' or 'no' response. Just try the following and see what happens.

Stand with your feet nine inches apart and parallel. Keep your spine straight and your head evenly weighted on top of your spine. To 'calibrate' yourself, think of the word 'Yes' – you will notice that your

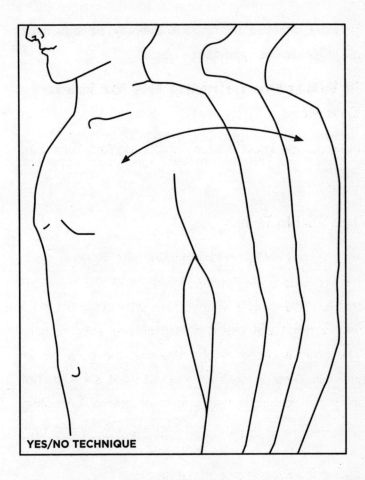

YES/NO TECHNIQUE

body will usually move slightly forwards. Then think of the word 'No' – your body will usually move backwards. Sometimes it does the opposite, so take that as your calibration for the day. It can change daily or even throughout the day, so this initial calibration is important.

Then ask yourself if something is OK, for example 'Is wheat OK for me?' or 'Is beer [or vodka or whatever you choose to drink] OK for me?' Notice which way your body moves to give you your answer.

All questions asked must have a yes or no response otherwise you will only receive confused responses or no response at all, so you must be specific in your questions.

The Smooth/Sticky Technique

An alternative method is to use your finger and thumb, rubbing them together very gently. Think 'Yes' and it should feel smooth; while thinking 'No' will make it feel rougher or 'different' in some noticeable way. If you have trouble using your finger and thumb, then use a credit card and rub it gently on its smooth side. 'Yes' will be easy and 'No' will have more friction and feel 'sticky'.

You can test pretty much anything utilizing this method.

SMOOTH/STICKY TECHNIQUE

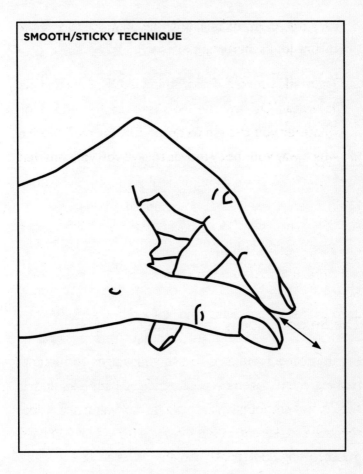

Note

Always end on a positive note, even if it is only thinking the word 'Yes' and moving forward or with a smooth or positive response to the finger rub. Avoid ending on a negative as this may influence your state for a few hours.

This is a truly amazing technique. If you are able to make it habitual, and in the main eat or drink only what your body tells you is OK for you, then the results for your well-being will be huge and you will have much more energy and vitality.

You can also test just about anything with this method, not only things you eat and drink. Try it … the worst that can happen is you will get no response.

I have discovered with my clients that toothpastes, hair products, makeup, clothes, work environments and even abstract things such as vapours from carpets or a new car can cause problems, and sometimes serious ones. Anecdotally I had one client who had chronic migraines that turned out to be caused by the leather car seats in his new car. Luckily he was able to change the lease, and had no further problems as soon as he'd replaced his car.

Just the Tonic

OK, so, unless you are very rare and have a toxic reaction to water, you can use the following technique on your next night out.

By drinking water between drinks you are allowing your body to pace itself in a much more effective way. Your liver and kidneys will have much less of a workload to deal with and you will also be reducing the chances of becoming dehydrated, which is an issue for developing not just hangovers but also what is known as PR or Psychological Reversal (for more about this, see page 129). And being dehydrated just isn't good for you in any case. Your stomach will also become more attuned to a full feeling so you are less likely to eat rubbish food, to fill the gap.

Water is good for you; you are made up mostly of water, anyway, so you can think of it as just topping yourself up with more of 'you'.

All water – 'Adam's ale', 'Corporation Pop' or whatever you choose to call it – is fine, whether it is from a tap or bottle, still or fizzy, soda or tonic. Just make sure you keep hydrated. The benefits are endless, as are the consequences of becoming dehydrated. Also, think about this: if you drink water on a 1:1 ratio with your normal alcoholic drink, you could save potentially 50 per cent of your money on a night out. You will also feel and look much better in the morning, especially your skin and eyes. Hangovers are likely to be less pounding. Can you see the value in drinking water yet?

Negativity and How to Stay Out of It

There is a joke I tell when doing Meridian Therapy trainings and it goes like this:

A client walks into a therapist's office and says, 'I feel really bad, out of sorts, you know? … Really negative.' The therapist does some tapping and some other stuff and then asks the client, 'How do you feel now?''Oh, much better,' replies the client. 'Are you sure?' asks the therapist. 'Oh yes, I'm positive,' responds the client.

Although this is just a joke (*good or bad is for you to decide*), it is not that far from the truth. We can show, using a standard electrician's multi-meter set on millivolts (mV), that the human body can be measured like a battery, and shows a positive or negative reading depending on what's going on with it. This is an empirical measurement that cannot be faked, controlled or put down to the placebo effect. Once a measured negative state is treated using Meridian Therapy and the individual is retested with the multi-meter it will then register, in most cases, a positive reading. Again this effect has to be placebo free, as the multi-meter is just that: a measuring device free of opinion or bias. It just gives numbers.

OK, cool … so what does this mean?

Psychological Reversal

Callahan's first discovery in Meridian Therapy was the concept of what he termed 'Psychological Reversal' (or PR, to give it its abbreviated form). He noted that in some cases clients did not respond to treatment of any form, and could not, in the case of kinesiology, be muscle-tested accurately; thus, the information being gathered by the practitioner would be invalidated.

We have since learned that there are different levels of PR and, while any of these levels remains active, then it is unlikely any treatment will achieve what it is meant to. Although it is termed *Psychological* Reversal, it has *physical* ramifications, too. One example is a bone fracture that will not heal. In a good example of conventional orthodox medicine and complementary therapies sharing common ground, surgeons now place battery packs either side of a fracture site to create the correct current flow, which will enable the PR to be eliminated locally and allow the fracture to heal. We know that all a person has to do is tap the side of their hand to achieve a similar effect, but it's an encouraging sign whenever conventional and complementary therapies work side by side.

PR is a state we can flip into at any time without warning, and you can have no idea you are in that state unless you measure it, as mentioned, with a multi-meter. There are other signs that we may be in PR. Some of these are:

- *TFT (and other treatments) don't work*

- *We reverse our words, concepts, numbers*

- *Dyslexia*

- *Irritability, negativity, 'bad moods'*

- *Self-sabotage*

- *Negative self-talk*

- *Procrastination*

- *Mental or creative blocks.*

To put it simply, PR is almost like having your batteries put in backwards, so nothing seems to work properly. Once the reversal is corrected, it is like having the batteries put in the correct way round so that everything seems to function properly again. Another element that may cause or significantly contribute to a PR state is the effect of toxins on our system – hence the value of being able to use the Yes/No technique to ascertain if something is OK for you or not.

There are several ways to combat PR and to keep it at bay. These are:

1. **Tapping the PR points (the side of your hand and under your nose, in the main)**

2. **Using positive affirmations**

3. **Using Bach Flower Rescue Remedy**

4. **Keeping well hydrated.**

That last one I discovered while on a diving trip to the Red Sea. When you dive you breathe compressed air, which dehydrates you, so the dive masters advise you to drink plenty of water pre- and post-dive, as being dehydrated can cause a number of health issues and is a significant contributor to decompression sickness, also known as 'the bends'. Hmm ... there's a thought: we often refer to getting drunk as 'going on a bender ...'

Anyway, I digress. During the week's diving I tested the divers on a multi-meter pre- and post-dive, and in most cases – not all, but most – the post-dive readings showed a minus number on the millivolts on the multi-meter. I tested the divers a few minutes later, after they had rehydrated by drinking some water, and again in most cases they had reverted to showing positive millivolts. I asked those who had not drunk any water to tap the side of their hand and then I also retested them, and this time everyone displayed a positive millivolts reading. This was only a small sample and is mainly anecdotal, but after a week of testing I was convinced this was not just a coincidence.

It seems to me that the best way to avoid PR (and all its associated negativity) is to adopt a preventative philosophy. The following exercises will allow you to do just that.

First, and simplest, is to keep hydrated. As mentioned earlier, think about alternating drinks so you are having a glass of water between each alcoholic drink.

Secondly, keep out of PR by using the following exercise. The worst that will happen is that you will feel good 'for no reason at all'.

- **Tap (karate chop) on the side of your hand, point and say:**

  'I want to be …' (in control/fit/healthy or whatever you choose to say)

  'I can be …'

  'I will be …'

  'I am …'

  'I'm OK.'

- **Tap under your nose 30 times**

- **Tap your chin 30 times**

- **Tap your other hand and say:**

  'I want to feel even better.'

  'I can feel even better.'

  'I will feel even better.'

  'I am going to feel even better.'

  'I'm OK.'

  'I'm more than OK.'

Note

You may notice at the end of this exercise that your hands may tingle or buzz. Try to think of something negative at this point and see what happens. Even if you can think of something negative, you should experience a state of total ambivalence towards it.

Thirdly, you can support all of this by occasionally taking Rescue Remedy. The Bach Flower website (see the Resources chapter, page 160) gives you a full history and information about this healing therapy. It is also available from most pharmacies or online, and is available as a spray or as drops, an ointment or even pastilles. Using Rescue Remedy should be seen as a supplement to all the other techniques developed in this book.

Think of the tapping sequences as being like tapping keys on a keyboard in a specific sequence to eliminate a computer virus, or at least stop it running for a period, safe in the knowledge that if it returns you can simply tap it away again, because you know the code to tap in to get rid of it. This is a very important point: random tapping will not eliminate the problems you are dealing with. You need to tap the specific code or sequence as outlined in the exercises explored in this chapter.

If you think of your body as a computer, and health issues, addictions or moods as bad programmes or viruses, creating negativity, then I hope you can see the value of being able to have control over these viruses, and being able to keep yourself virus-free.

Now, just as you would run a virus scan periodically on your PC, there is an exercise that enables you to do the same for yourself. Its origins come from applied kinesiology, but it has been adopted and modified slightly by Meridian Therapy systems. The exercise is called collarbone breathing.

Collarbone Breathing

First, find the 'knuckle' on the inner end of your collarbone, where it joins the top of the breastbone. There's one on each side. Then drop your fingers down about an inch, to the first soft space above your first rib. That's the collarbone point.

OK, now place the fingertips of one hand (either one, as you're going to do both anyway) and, once you have your fingertips in place, begin to tap the back of that hand with the fingertips of the other hand, tapping between the little finger and the ring finger knuckle. Continue to tap as you do this:

- **Take a deep breath in and hold it for a couple of seconds**

- **Release half the breath and hold for a couple of seconds**

- **Release all the breath and hold for a couple of seconds**

- **Take in half a breath and hold it for a couple of seconds**

- **Then breathe normally.**

Now bend your fingers and place your top knuckles where your fingertips were, making sure your thumb does not make any contact with your skin. Tap the same spot on the back of your hand, and repeat the breathing exercise as you continue to tap.

Once you've done that, move your hand across to the other collarbone point and, using your top knuckles again, tap as you do the breathing.

Once that is complete, open your hand so that your fingertips are now touching the collarbone point, and repeat the tapping and the breathing pattern again.

That's one half of the exercise done; now repeat it on the other hand, using exactly the same hand positions, tapping and breathing, until the exercise is complete.

The whole sequence should take a maximum of 2 minutes to complete. I highly recommend doing it as a daily exercise, with the best time being first thing in the morning. It achieves a few things simultaneously: it clears your head of all the junk so you are able to focus. It helps eliminate toxins built up in the system. It provides an energy boost to your meridian system. It makes you feel calm (like you have had a 20-minute meditation). All of this in a 2-minute exercise. Why would you choose not to do it?

Reverse Breathing

Another rapid technique I sometimes use, and get clients to use, is a pattern-breaking exercise that I call *reverse breathing*. It works on the principle that the brain is expecting one thing to happen, and you do the opposite.

We all normally breathe in through our noses and out through our mouths. This is an automatic pattern that we do without any apparent thought. So if we simply break the pattern by reversing it and breathing in forcefully through our mouths, and forcefully out through our noses several times, it seems to throw the brain a bit of a curveball and stops whatever was going to happen from happening.

I have given this technique to a number of clients who suffer from panic attacks, and they have offered feedback to me that it is very empowering to have such a simple exercise at their disposal.

Simple, but effective stuff … Yes?

Anchoring

This is a very useful exercise that we all do naturally. Neuro-Linguistic Programming (NLP) has, however, looked at the strategy of how we anchor states, then has modelled it and developed some very simple but elegant methodologies to enable you to use it selectively, in the areas of your life where it may be most beneficial.

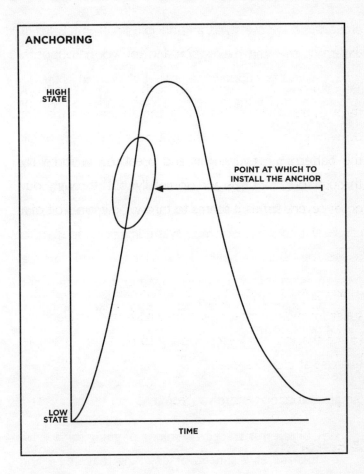

Anchors can be visual, auditory, kinaesthetic, olfactory or gustatory, or a combination of any or all of these.

Most, if not all, anchors end up with a kinaesthetic (feeling) response. We see an image, hear a song, smell a food or imagine slaking our thirst and we get a feeling, a reaction internally, that can make us feel either good or bad. As I have said, this happens naturally but we can artificially create or amplify these feelings so we can have them 'on tap', so to speak.

> **Think of a food or drink that you know would make you feel sick if you ate or drank it. OK, now imagine ingesting it, being forced to take it down your throat. Feel it coating your mouth and imagine the smell of it, too. Really amplify the sensations until you feel repulsion. Now squeeze together the thumb and little finger of your left hand as you reach the height of repulsion.**

Note

It's good to stop before you vomit. ☺

> **OK, break this state by thinking of going for a drive or looking at a sunset, or anything that's new and different. Now squeeze together the thumb and little finger of your left hand again and see what happens. If you immediately get that feeling of repulsion, congratulations: you have just installed an anchor, with squeezing the finger and thumb of your left hand being the trigger that fires it off.**

Now let's do the same thing again, but this time think of something you desire, or something positive.

Note

It is always advisable to finish on a positive and resourceful anchor; otherwise you could end up walking around feeling bad for no reason.

So now think of something you really want, and imagine having it. Imagine how you would feel. What would you say to yourself and what would you see? Now amplify everything, all the sensations, until the feelings grow and grow (*if you're not smiling … it isn't working*). Boost those feelings even more, and then squeeze the thumb and index finger together as you feel really good.

Then stop and break that state by thinking of something else.

Now fire off the positive anchor you have just installed, and see and feel that you can feel really good easily and for no other reason than that you choose to. Oh, and it is calorie-free, costs nothing and the only side-effect is feeling good. Imagine what it would be like if you could get drunk on good feelings alone? Maybe even anchor that! ☺

FINGER AND THUMB SQUEEZING

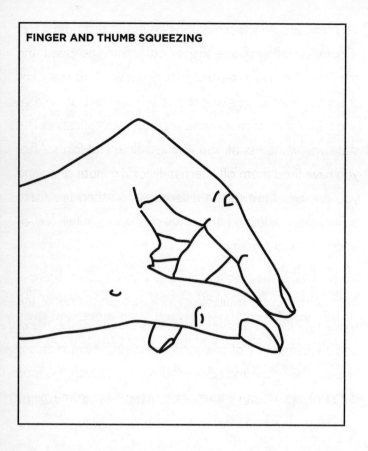

You can then think other good stuff and add it to the mix of the first anchor. We call this method *stacking anchors*, and there is no limit to how many you can have. I personally tend to stack three to five at a time so as not to overwhelm myself. But you can set your own limits, as it is your choice and under your control.

You can also use a technique called *collapsing anchors*. This is done by creating one anchor on one trigger point and then another on a separate trigger point. You then fire them off alternately, giving the state you want to achieve and have more of more time and more amplification. The state you want less of, you give less time and focus. After you have fired them off alternately for a minute or so and you can really notice the difference, you then fire them off together and find that one state will cancel out or collapse the other one.

If you really want to get into anchoring then there a host of resources available on the net or in one of the many NLP books. I have covered just some of the basics and fundamentals of anchoring, done my way, that any layperson can use and achieve some results with. YouTube is full of examples of anchoring techniques, some being very impressive and some less so.

Imagine how good it would feel to be able to control your feelings and emotional states with such a simple action as squeezing your finger and thumb. Or you can get creative with your own method, which I would encourage!

'Think how good it would feel to have that control right now.'

Then anchor it ☺

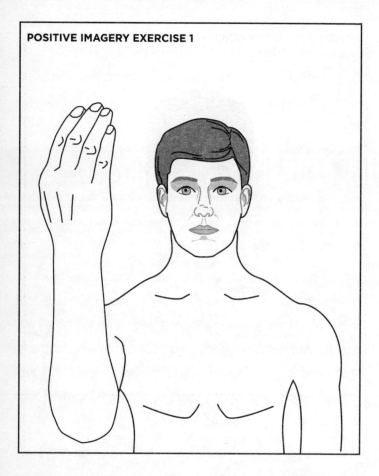

POSITIVE IMAGERY EXERCISE 1

Positive Imagery

How do we create horrible thoughts that make us feel bad? Well, in the main we make up bad pictures in our mind and, as we visualize, we catastrophize a situation and

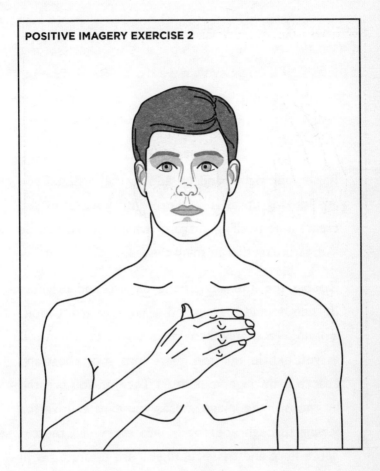

POSITIVE IMAGERY EXERCISE 2

subsequently feel bad. This, in NLP terms, is what we refer to as a 'strategy'; it is not, however, a very useful one. Well, actually, the strategy works very elegantly whether we think of a good outcome or a bad one. Yet we all seem

145

to be able to do the negative one more easily. How is this the case? I would suggest it's because we have *practised* it more. So, I thought, what if we did the same thing but with good feelings? Oh, and practise it, too, so we get good at it. The following exercise is the result. Practise it now.

> Raise your right hand up and to the right, so you are looking up at it … Look into your palm and create a compelling image of what you want to be like, assuming that nothing can fail.
>
> Double the intensity of the picture and brighten it. Then double it again and again … when it looks amazing – and only then – take a deep breath in and, as you exhale, pull the image into your chest and absorb it through your heart. Then, as you breathe in, intensify the image and, as you exhale, drive the feeling through your body into every cell, muscle, nerve fibre and tissue, until you are saturated with the good feeling. Then repeat with another good image.

Do this as often as you like … after all, who can ever have enough good feelings?

A Winding-down Exercise, Part I: Relaxation Breathing

People often say they need a drink to 'wind down' after work or if they have been in a stressful situation. That's OK unless it is your only option and you 'have to' have that drink ... just like you have to blink. That's getting close to an addiction where you have little or no control. So here is a simple one-minute technique to relax you totally.

Touch each of the following points with two fingers, breathing slowly in through your nose and out through your mouth:

- **Top of head (on the crown of the head)**

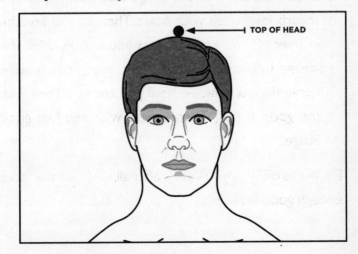

TOP OF HEAD

• Above your eye

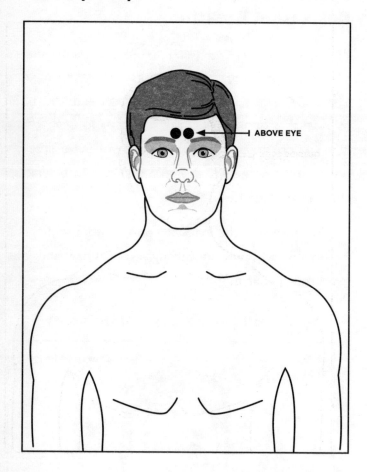

ABOVE EYE

- **Side of the eye**

OUTSIDE EDGE
OF EYE

- **Under the eye**

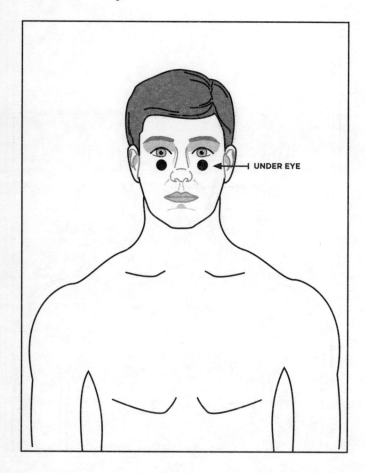

UNDER EYE

- ## Top and bottom lip

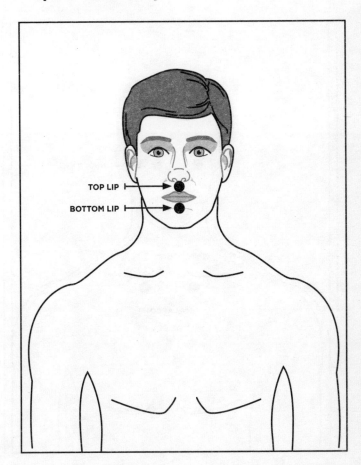

- **Under your collarbones**

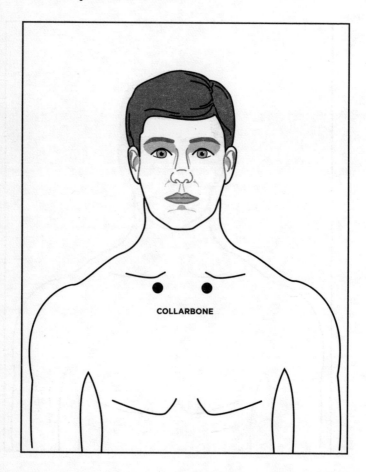

COLLARBONE

- ## Under the arms 10 cm down

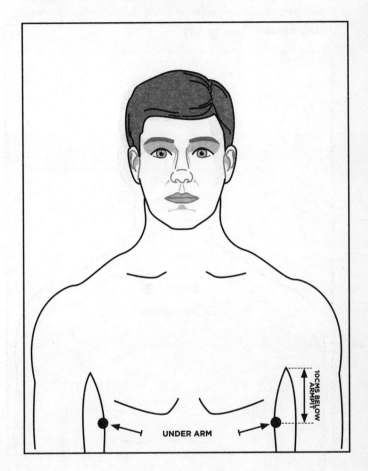

- **Middle of your forehead between your eyebrows (breathe in and out three times as you touch this spot)**

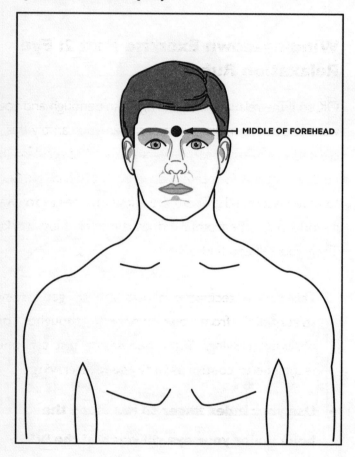

MIDDLE OF FOREHEAD

This simple exercise is a very nice 'chill pill'; it's calorie-free and cannot do anything but relax you.

Winding-down Exercise Part 2: Eye Relaxation Rub

OK, so if the relaxation breathing wasn't enough and you want to achieve mega-chill status, then you can try this. I created this exercise some years ago, kind of accidentally. I did not set out to create what it does, but I am pleased to have discovered it. There are a few theories as to why it works, but to be truthful it doesn't matter; it just works. Try it yourself and find out.

> This simple technique allows you to get instant stress-relief from any worrying thoughts or obsessive cravings. Some people use just this one technique to control anxiety and food cravings.

- **Use your index finger to rub along the bone under your eye till you feel the 'V' indentation in the eye-socket bone.**

- **Place a finger each side of this 'V'.**

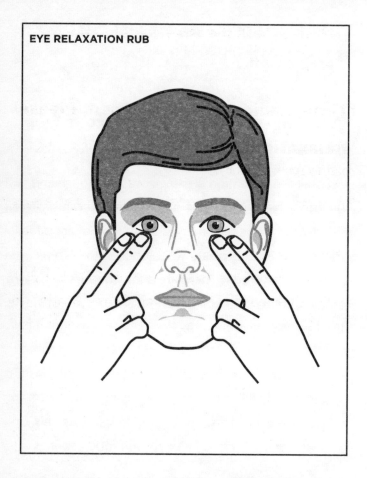

EYE RELAXATION RUB

- **Massage in a small circle one way, then the other way.**

- **Massage it back the other way but with twice the pressure.**

- **Massage back the other way but take the pressure off.**

'Time, Ladies and Gentlemen, Please'

Well, that's it; book's over … time to move on … hit the road. You've had your fill …

And now you have had your fill of thoughts, stories, facts and stats and techniques, it really is 'time'. You now have an array of techniques and thoughts and ideas, which if you use them will put you fully back in control of your alcohol consumption. Time to choose, then, what to do with the knowledge you now have and the wisdom it has given you.

It is said that being aware that a tomato is actually a fruit is knowledge … not putting it into your fruit salad is wisdom. Which path will you take? Will you head on back down the road you were on before? Perhaps you will take a wiser path and occasionally allow yourself to be carried along the road of life by a wagon, to allow your system to rest and enable yourself to recover, so that when you really do decide to enjoy yourself, you do really enjoy yourself.

You need to choose, to decide to change. I steal a quote from the author's note of my last book, which I will repeat here.

Trying to change something by 100 per cent will usually lead to failure … it is too big. However, you can change 100 things by 1 per cent and that is what will make the difference. The small things make the big difference.

Enjoy the difference you can have in your life now … and maybe I'll see you – in control – in the bar sometime. ☺

– Kevin Laye *(A Positive Drinker)*

Further Reading and Resources

I highly recommend the following books:

The Mind/Body Prescription by John Sarno MD (Little, Brown, 2007)

Tapping the Healer Within by Dr Roger Callahan (McGraw-Hill, 2002)

Monsters and Magical Sticks by Dr Stephen Heller and Terry Steele (New Falcon, 2001)

Positive Shrinking by Kevin Laye (Hay House, 2010)

You Can Have What You Want by Michael Neill (Hay House, 2009)

Change Your Life in Seven Days by Paul McKenna (Bantam, 2010)

Jonathan Livingston Seagull by Richard Bach (Element, 2005)

Websites

www.kevinlaye.co.uk

www.positiveshrinking.co.uk

www.cameltrain.co.uk

www.2calm.com

www.emofree.com

www.paulmckenna.com

www.atft.org

www.metachangework.co.uk

www.rescueremedy.com

www.bach-flowers.co.uk

Testimonial

In giving Kevin this testimonial, I would first like to outline my relationship with alcohol and how it affected my life and health – this brings into context the amazing help I received from Kevin Laye and how it is slowly changing my life. That is not to say it has been easy – far from it – but it has been one of the most worthwhile and life-saving events of my 60-odd years on this planet.

Both my parents were chronic alcoholics. I grew up believing that I, too, would follow the same path, until I was in my late teens. I met my ex-husband and told myself I would never drink and would begin a fantastic family life with children and a husband. Knight on white charger included!

This worked well until I was around 32, when my marriage ended and I was left with four children under the age of 11. So I began to buy what was then called a 'double double' – that is, 4 units of whisky. I'd wait until the kids were in bed and secretly drink it for a treat!

Then, some years later on a caravanning holiday with a divorced friend and her children, when the kids were settled we drank tea – laced with whisky. Never got drunk, but once again, a treat! Some three years later my 'double double' had become a whole bottle of whisky a week. I was at university then and spoke to an alcohol counsellor, who told me not to be silly, I was using it as a crutch and it would cease when I felt better. Well, talk about giving someone permission!

The years rolled on – I had a steady job, bought a house and the kids grew up and gradually all went to university. All through this, I drank, when they were in bed, when they were staying at their dad's, or when they were out for the night. Alcohol, like any addiction, crept up on me. My one saving grace was that I never drank in the day. This probably saved my health, my job and my life.

As time went on and I was living alone, I got worse. Every upset, every hard day's work became 'rewarded'.

I slowly became ill. I had asthma, high blood pressure, depression and, worst of all, gout. I never told my GP I drank, and he never asked.

In desperation I joined AA, and although I still use some of the help I received there, it wasn't for me. I now look back on this time and think how sad and lonely I was, though far too proud to accept the help I was offered.

I attended an NLP course in London with Richard Bandler and Paul McKenna. I had never heard of NLP before. The secret drinking continued. At night in my hotel room I would order lots of room service – alcohol, of course. By then I thought I would never recover and was just like my parents. I truly forgot about the good mum I was and the achievements I had made in my life. That's alcohol for you – it takes away your being and your soul and leaves you with nothing. If you let it.

So, all in all, 27 years of drinking and nowhere to go. That is, until I rang the Paul McKenna helpline after the course. They put me in touch with Kevin Laye, who saw me and treated me with Thought Field Therapy (TFT) and hypnosis. I hadn't heard of TFT before but agreed to do the tapping as shown.

At first I didn't drink for over three months. My body began to recover and I really thought I had cracked it. I was so grateful to Kevin. Then, something stressful occurred and I began again. I telephoned Kevin, who saw me again. I was drinking vodka and he, once more, patiently helped me. No more alcohol for another while, and then the same thing happened again. Yet again, a very difficult family event turned me to drink, or so I told myself. At that time, I threw away the TFT Success Booklet! I told myself 'tapping was rubbish.' Addictions give you loads of room for excuses!

Slowly, the penny was beginning to drop – every time I felt stressed and bad about something, I began drinking. So, feeling miserable, humiliated and extremely embarrassed, once more I contacted Kevin, thinking 'One of these days, he's going to tell me to get lost.' But he didn't. The last treatment I received was eight weeks ago. This time, I feel so different, more in control. I won't lie and say drinking never enters my head, although never when shopping. I sail past the alcohol displays without a thought. It is events that are my triggers. For example, I'm a bit of a political animal. At the last election but one I became very drunk when Labour won. I sat watching the returns this time and thought to myself, 'Oh, no, you don't.' Who cares who wins? What is important is my sobriety.

Recently I had a difficult time and realized that *everyone* has bad times. I did not drink on it and have no intention of doing so. I went and 'tapped' instead until it passed, which was remarkably quickly.

I don't need alcohol as a crutch anymore. Kevin has helped me eradicate the past through NLP, TFT and hypnosis. Believe me, it works. A favourite saying I learned in AA is, 'It works if you work it, it won't if you don't.' How true.

So, am I well – in my head? Yes. In my body? Not yet. Some 27 years of abuse takes time to disappear – but it will, with time. The only treat I need is to be proud of what I have achieved and am still achieving. Try it for yourself: it is life-changing.

I truly cannot thank Kevin Laye enough. He has been patient, encouraging, understanding and knowing. He made me feel confident that I could crack this by simply saying little, helping when asked and keeping in touch now and then, which means a lot. I no longer view myself as a helpless drunk who 'can't help it'. With Kevin Laye's amazing help I am recovering and sober. It is truly a great place to be. What has Kevin done that others couldn't? Not judged, been there and worked his magic. That magic includes helping me see the light – wow!

Love,

Sue x

Notes

Notes

Notes

Notes

Titles of Related Interest

Cosmic Ordering for Beginners,
by Barbel Mohr

How to Become a Money Magnet,
by Marie-Claire Carlyle

Matrix Reimprinting,
by Karl Dawson & Sasha Allenby

One-Minute Mystic,
by Simon Parke

Positive Shrinking,
by Kevin Laye

The Power of No,
by Beth Wareham

Tapping for Life,
by Janet Thomson

We hope you enjoyed this Hay House book.
If you would like to receive a free catalogue featuring additional
Hay House books and products, or if you would like information
about the Hay Foundation, please contact:

Hay House UK Ltd
292B Kensal Road • London W10 5BE
Tel: (44) 20 8962 1230; Fax: (44) 20 8962 1239
www.hayhouse.co.uk

***

Published and distributed in the United States of America by:
Hay House, Inc. • PO Box 5100 • Carlsbad, CA 92018-5100
Tel: (1) 760 431 7695 or (1) 800 654 5126;
Fax: (1) 760 431 6948 or (1) 800 650 5115
www.hayhouse.com

***

Published and distributed in Australia by:
Hay House Australia Ltd • 18/36 Ralph Street • Alexandria, NSW 2015
Tel: (61) 2 9669 4299, Fax: (61) 2 9669 4144
www.hayhouse.com.au

***

Published and distributed in the Republic of South Africa by:
Hay House SA (Pty) Ltd • PO Box 990 • Witkoppen 2068
Tel/Fax: (27) 11 467 8904
www.hayhouse.co.za

***

Published and distributed in India by:
Hay House Publishers India • Muskaan Complex • Plot No.3
B-2• Vasant Kunj • New Delhi - 110 070
Tel: (91) 11 41761620; Fax: (91) 11 41761630
www.hayhouse.co.in

***

Distributed in Canada by:
Raincoast • 9050 Shaughnessy St • Vancouver, BC V6P 6E5
Tel: (1) 604 323 7100
Fax: (1) 604 323 2600

***

Sign up via the Hay House UK website to receive the Hay House
online newsletter and stay informed about what's going on with your
favourite authors. You'll receive bimonthly announcements
about discounts and offers, special events, product highlights,
free excerpts, giveaways, and more!
www.hayhouse.co.uk

JOIN THE HAY HOUSE FAMILY

As the leading self-help, mind, body and spirit publisher in the UK, we'd like to welcome you to our family so that you can enjoy all the benefits our website has to offer.

 EXTRACTS from a selection of your favourite author titles

 COMPETITIONS, PRIZES & SPECIAL OFFERS Win extracts, money off, downloads and so much more

 LISTEN to a range of radio interviews and our latest audio publications

 **CELEBRATE YOUR BIRTHDAY** An inspiring gift will be sent your way

 LATEST NEWS Keep up with the latest news from and about our authors

 ATTEND OUR AUTHOR EVENTS Be the first to hear about our author events

 iPHONE APPS Download your favourite app for your iPhone

 HAY HOUSE INFORMATION Ask us anything, all enquiries answered

join us online at **www.hayhouse.co.uk**

292B Kensal Road, London W10 5BE
T: 020 8962 1230 E: info@hayhouse.co.uk